Diving & Snorkeling

Fiji

Casey Mahaney & Astrid Witte Mahaney

LONELY PLANET PUBLICATIONS
Melbourne • Oakland • London • Paris

Diving & Snorkeling Fiji
- A Lonely Planet Pisces Book

2nd Edition – November 2000
1st Edition – 1993 Gulf Publishing Company

Published by
Lonely Planet Publications
90 Maribyrnong St., Footscray, Victoria, 3011, Australia

Other offices
150 Linden Street, Oakland, California 94607, USA
10a Spring Place, London NW5 3BH, UK
1 rue du Dahomey, 75011 Paris, France

Photographs
All photographs, including covers, by Casey Mahaney &
Astrid Witte Mahaney unless otherwise noted

Front cover photograph
Gazing through the "Window of Dreams," Namena

Back cover photographs
Fijian guitarists in colorful sulus
Flossing with a cleaner shrimp in Namena
Seeing the light at Broken Stone on the
    Great Astrolabe Reef

Most of the images in this guide are available for
    licensing from **Lonely Planet Images**
email: lpi@lonelyplanet.com.au

ISBN 1 86442 771 9

text & maps © Lonely Planet 2000
photographs © photographers as indicated 2000
illustration © Lonely Planet 2000
dive site maps are Transverse Mercator projection

LONELY PLANET and the Lonely Planet logo are
trademarks of Lonely Planet Publications Pty Ltd.

Printed by H&Y Printing Ltd., Hong Kong

Contents

Diving in Fiji   33

Viti Levu Dive Sites   39

Northern Viti Levu   39

Southern Viti Levu   46

Mamanuca Group Dive Sites   56

Yasawa Group Dive Sites   62

Vanua Levu & Namena Dive Sites   66

Vanua Levu   66

Authors

Casey Mahaney & Astrid Witte Mahaney

Casey Mahaney and Astrid Witte Mahaney are internationally published photojournalists who specialize in underwater photography. They are the authors of five marine life identification guides and numerous scuba travel and destination guides. Casey and Astrid have lived in Hawaii and throughout the South Pacific for more than 15 years, spending weeks and sometimes months in Fiji every year for more than five years. Having introduced thousands of divers to the magic of Pacific reefs, they now specialize in escorted live-aboard dive tours to Fiji and other exotic destinations. Find them on the internet at www.bluekirio.com.

From the Authors

So many people helped make this guide possible—from the taxi driver who "rescued us" when the road was flooded, to the strong Fijians who helped us lug our heavy camera equipment, to the dive operators and divemasters who provided us with contact information and answers to our many questions. We would like to say *vinaka* (thank you) to all of them.

We particularly want to thank those whose support and generous contributions of knowledge, dive vessels and accommodations helped make this guide as complete and accurate as possible. Special thanks to: Gary Alford, Bob and Rena Forster and the staff at Dive Kadavu and Jona's Paradise Resort; Lance Millar; the Douglas family; Carolyn Ah Koy; Ra Divers' legendary divemaster Papu; Rob Barrel, Cat Holloway and their devoted crew aboard Nai'a; the Fiji Aggressor crew; George Taylor and the dive staff at Marlin Bay Resort; John Gray, his family and the staff at Wananavu Beach Resort; Tony Cottrell and the dive staff from Subsurface; the Fiji Tourist Bureau; Helen Sykes and Stuart Gow from Resort Support; Dan Grenier and Mike Trussell from Crystal Divers; the staff at Lomaloma Resort; dive instructor Jason Smith; Brandon Cole, Air Fiji; Sunflower Airlines; and the staff at Tokatoka Resort.

Diving, talking and e-mailing with all of you has been a true pleasure. We hope to see each of you again soon!

Photography Notes

Underwater, Casey and Astrid use a variety of cameras and formats. For macro and close-up photography they use the Nikon 8008s and N90s fitted with either a 105mm or 60mm lens in an Ikelite housing. For wide-angle photography they prefer to shoot the 20mm and 14mm lenses in a Nexus housing or use Nikonos III and V cameras with a 15mm lens. Topside, they work with their Nikon cameras and a wider variety of lenses, including zoom lenses. They prefer Fujichrome slide films such as Velvia, Provia and Sensia II for their brilliant color saturation.

Contributing Photographers

Casey Mahaney and Astrid Witte Mahaney took most of the photographs in this book. Thanks also to Roslyn Bullas, Sarah Hubbard and Bill Kritzberg for their photo contributions.

From the Publisher

This second edition was published in Lonely Planet's U.S. office under the guidance of Roslyn Bullas, the "Divemaster" of Pisces Books. From the coral-encrusted Fish Tank, David "Fish Story" Lauterborn edited the text and photos with buddy checks from Sarah "Sunfish" Hubbard and China "Slender Wrasse" Williams. "Super Grouper" Emily Douglas designed the cover and book with assistance from Ruth "Rainbow Runner" Askevold. Navigating the nautical charts was cartographer Mary Hagemann, who created the maps, with assistance from Sara Nelson and John Spelman. Alex Guilbert supervised map production. Mick Weldon illustrated the Kadavu sidebar. Lindsay Brown reviewed the Marine Life section for scientific accuracy. Portions of the text were adapted from Lonely Planet's *Fiji*.

Pisces Pre-Dive Safety Guidelines

Before embarking on a scuba diving, skin diving or snorkeling trip, carefully consider the following to help ensure a safe and enjoyable experience:

- Possess a current diving certification card from a recognized scuba diving instructional agency (if scuba diving)
- Be sure you are healthy and feel comfortable diving
- Obtain reliable information about physical and environmental conditions at the dive site (e.g., from a reputable local dive operation)
- Be aware of local laws, regulations and etiquette about marine life and environment
- Dive at sites within your experience level; if possible, engage the services of a competent, professionally trained dive instructor or divemaster

Underwater conditions vary significantly from one region, or even site, to another. Seasonal changes can significantly alter site and dive conditions. These differences influence the way divers dress for a dive and what diving techniques they use.

There are special requirements for diving in any area, regardless of location. Before your dive, ask about environmental characteristics that can affect your diving and how trained local divers deal with these considerations.

Warning & Request

Things change—dive site conditions, regulations, topside information. Nothing stays the same for long. Your feedback on this book will be used to help update and improve the next edition. Excerpts from your correspondence may appear in *Planet Talk*, our quarterly newsletter, or *Comet*, our monthly email newsletter. Please let us know if you do not want your letter published or your name acknowledged.

Correspondence can be addressed to:
Lonely Planet Publications
Pisces Books
150 Linden Street
Oakland, CA 94607
email: pisces@lonelyplanet.com

Introduction

Once known as the dreaded "Cannibal Isles," Fiji today is renowned for the friendliness of its people. Taught from an early age to treasure family and friendship, Fijians welcome visitors with warm smiles and sincere hospitality, whether you are checking into a 5-star dive resort or budget backpacker lodge or visiting one of their villages.

In addition to its welcoming people, the archipelago boasts a stunning landscape of lush tropical islands, white-sand beaches and azure lagoons, as well as world-class diving.

Celebrated as the soft-coral capital of the world, Fiji is blessed with an abundance of overwhelmingly colorful reefs, walls and remote seamounts. Divers are also awed by frequent pelagic encounters, a dazzling array of more than 1,000 tropical fish species and many interesting and unusual invertebrates.

Fiji's largest island, Viti Levu is home to the capital, Suva, as well as the town of Nadi (pronounced NAN-di), where international flights typically arrive. Most of the region's luxury resorts are near Nadi—along the sunny west and southwest coasts of Viti Levu and in the neighboring Mamanuca Group islands. Numerous

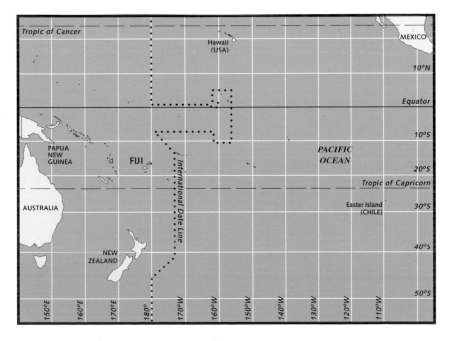

smaller resorts are scattered throughout the archipelago, many catering specifically to divers. As some of Fiji's prime dive sites are rather remote, live-aboards have also become a popular option.

Since Fiji comprises more than 300 islands spanning some 1.3 million sq km (500,000 sq miles) of the South Pacific, it would be impractical to list every dive site in the country. This book covers the regions of most interest to divers, including the north and south coasts and offshore islands of **Viti Levu**, the **Mamanuca Group**, the **Yasawa Group**, **Vanua Levu & Namena**, **Taveuni**, the **Kadavu Group & the Great Astrolabe Reef**, the vast region of **Bligh Water**, the **Lomaiviti Group** and the accessible islands of the **Lau Group**.

You'll find specific information on 74 of Fiji's best sites, including location, depth, access and recommended diving expertise. You'll also learn about each site's underwater terrain and the marine life you may encounter. The Marine Life section even offers a preview of Fiji's most common vertebrates and invertebrates. While the book is not intended as a stand-alone travel guide, the Overview and Practicalities sections provide useful information about the islands, and the Activities & Attractions section offers tips on topside pursuits.

Be sure to plan plenty of time to explore and enjoy!

ROSLYN BULLAS

Fijian children romp in the surf on Caqelai Island in the Lomaiviti Group.

Overview

One of the South Pacific's most cosmopolitan nations, the Republic of the Fiji Islands has a young, multiracial population approaching 800,000, the majority composed of indigenous Fijians (51%) and Fiji Indians (44%), with small numbers of Europeans, Chinese and other Pacific islanders. The country's capital, Suva, is the largest city in the South Pacific and home to nearly one-quarter of Fiji's population.

Three languages are spoken on the islands, and the archipelago is also a meeting ground of three of the world's great religions. Christianity, Hinduism and Islam are all practiced here in tolerance with one another.

Outside the cities, Fiji's economy remains primarily agrarian, and subsistence farming on a village level is still an important way of life for many islanders. The largest earner of hard currency is tourism, followed by sugar (the main export crop), gold, copra, tuna, ginger and cocoa.

Geography

Fiji lies on the international date line, approximately 2,100km (1,300 miles) north of New Zealand, 3,200km (2,000 miles) northeast of Australia and 5,000km (3,100 miles) southwest of Hawaii.

City streets give way to sugarcane fields in Fiji's outlying areas.

The archipelago's 332 islands span an area of some 1.3 million sq km (500,000 sq miles), but only about 18,300 sq km (7,100 sq miles) of it is dry land. Factor in the 1,100km (680 miles) of coastline fringed with countless kilometers of unspoiled reefs, and it's clear why Fiji is so popular with divers.

Geology

The Fijian islands fall into three geologic categories.

The larger, mountainous islands such as Viti Levu, Vanua Levu, Kadavu and Taveuni are volcanic in origin. They feature steep central ridges with prominent basaltic outcroppings and rivers that cascade down from the higher elevations, often in spectacular waterfalls.

Next are the smaller, low-elevation coral islands, which generally reach no more than 15m (50ft) above sea level. Often consisting of seductive white-sand beaches ringing blue lagoons, they embody the ideal of a romantic South Pacific paradise. Islands in the Lomaiviti Group are this type.

The third type is limestone-based and features jagged, pitted shorelines that drop abruptly into the sea. At sea level, the irregular shoreline is often undercut from years of wave action and weathering, offering interesting wall dives that typically include caves and caverns. This type tends to top out at 30m (100ft) and includes some of the Lau Group islands.

Thousands of miles of coral reef thread throughout these islands, the barrier reef being the most common type. Often encircling an island, such reefs form a protective barrier between the open sea and the island. If over time the island within this barrier sinks into its lagoon, the remaining circular reef is referred to as an atoll.

On the seaward side of a barrier reef, divers generally find sheer walls blanketed in coral and sea fans—though in areas prone to severe wave action, these walls can be quite barren, particularly in the shallows. Between the barrier reef and its island is often a lagoon. This is typically a calm, shallow body of water that may not have the best visibility, but often fas-

Intricate reefs are home to more than a thousand tropical fish species.

cinates divers with unusual marine life species and juveniles not generally seen elsewhere.

All barrier reefs have natural channels that during the tidal cycle allow seawater to enter the lagoon and then flush water back into the open ocean. Marked by strong currents, these passages are the most productive zones on the reef and rank among the prime dive sites. Lush coral gardens, sea fans, mantas, sharks and numerous other marine creatures abound here.

History

The first Fijian settlers are believed to have arrived from what is now Papua New Guinea at least 3,500 years ago. Another wave of Melanesians began arriving in 500 BC, followed by a final massive influx about 1,000 years ago.

The earliest known European to wander into Fijian waters was Dutch explorer Abel Tasman, while searching for new trading routes in 1643. Next to arrive was British explorer Captain James Cook, who sailed to Fiji in 1774 and anchored off a tiny island in the southern Lau Group. A more infamous passerby was Cook's countryman Captain William Bligh, whose exploration of Fiji was a direct result of the famed mutiny on the HMS *Bounty*.

On April 28, 1789, when the *Bounty* was in Tongan waters, the crew rebelled, setting adrift Bligh and 18 of his loyal men in a small open longboat with few provisions and no weapons. The nearest European settlement was Timor in the East Indies, 5,800km (3,600 miles) to the west. The long voyage took the hapless crew past Fiji, then called the "Cannibal Isles." Beating the odds, all but one arrived safely in Timor after 47 days at sea.

Traditional thatched *bures* are still a common sight throughout Fiji.

Considering his circumstances, Bligh made remarkably accurate and detailed observations as the longboat sailed between the two main islands of Viti Levu and Vanua Levu, through the passage now known as Bligh Water.

Not until the dawning of the 19th century did Europeans venture ashore in Fiji, many lured by potential profits from the sandalwood and *bêche-de-mer* trades. The addition of European greed to an already unstable and barbarous mix of tribal rivalries ushered in a disastrous period for Fiji.

It took less than 10 years to denude the forests of sandalwood. And bêche-de-mer, a shallow-water sea cucumber considered an aphrodisiac in Asia, was fished out within 20 years (see sidebar, page 69). The Fijian people did not fare much better. Disease introduced from the outside, including measles, reduced the population by nearly half over an 80-year period. By 1921 the indigenous population stood at 84,000, only 42% of the pre-discovery population.

When Fiji became a British Crown Colony in October of 1874, the United Kingdom was the world master of colonization. Partly by accident and partly by design, Fiji did well under the rule of the first British governor, who had experience in other colonies.

Sir Arthur Gordon realized the chiefdom system worked well, so rather than trying to govern from above, he ruled the country through the existing chiefs,

Trouble in Paradise

Ethnic tensions between indigenous Fijians and Fiji Indians stretch back to colonial times. Immediately following independence, however, the economy thrived, Fijians were optimistic and the different races appeared to mix well. But as the economy dipped, underlying tensions grew and eventually led to the 1987 military coups.

When the April '87 elections seated a new government that was considered Fiji Indian–dominated, 5,000 indigenous Fijians marched in protest, voicing their fears of losing land rights and of Fiji Indian political and economic domination. On May 14, only a month after the elections, Lieutenant Colonel Sitiveni Rabuka led a surprise invasion of parliament by armed soldiers. He took over the government in a bloodless coup and later declared himself head of state, appointing a new council of ministers that included army officers and leaders of the divisive Taukei movement.

In 1991 Rabuka gave up his military career to pursue politics full time. To suit his ambitions, he became increasingly populist and was appointed prime minister in 1992. The new government faced a faltering economy that was still recovering from the drastic consequences of the coups. Hurricane Kina in 1993 added to Fiji's woes.

In the late '90s the economy weathered the Asian financial crisis and a prolonged drought, and tourism flourished. A more inclusive constitution was drawn up in 1997, and Mahendra Chaudhry was elected the first Fiji Indian prime minister in May 1999— seeming signs of growing ethnic parity.

But on May 19, 2000, armed civilian rebels stormed the parliament and took Chaudhry and most of his cabinet hostage. The coup leader, George Speight, who claimed to represent indigenous Fijians' concerns about native land rights and political power, demanded a new constitution, as well as a new government, prime minister and president of his choice. A long-term solution to the tensions remains elusive.

whose communal land he protected from ever being sold. Today indigenous Fijians remain in control of more than 80% of the land.

To keep the peace, Gordon also exempted Fijians from working on European plantations, instead turning to indentured Indian workers as a solution. Between 1879 and 1916, 63,000 Indians arrived in Fiji to work out 10-year contracts. More than half stayed once their contracts expired. These Indian workers, without access to communal Fijian lands, either continued farming on small leased plots or went into business. Today the majority of Fiji's businesses are Indian owned and managed.

Fiji gained independence from Britain in 1970. Following two coups in 1987, Fiji abandoned its parliamentary government and declared itself a republic.

Diving History

Recreational sport diving geared up in Fiji in the 1970s. Each region had its own pioneers: Dave and Lorraine Evans started Scuba Hire in Suva and Pacific Harbour on Viti Levu; Ric Cammick of Dive Taveuni explored the Taveuni area, discovering such legendary sites as the Great White Wall; the Douglas family helped explore the region around Matagi and northern Lau; and Bob and Rena Forster were the first to open up Kadavu to diving.

Word of Fiji's fabulous reefs spread as dive magazines ran colorful photos of magnificent soft corals. The archipelago was christened the soft-coral capital of the world and quickly became a top exotic dive travel destination.

Over the years, new dive operators have sprung up throughout Fiji. Now long retired, the *Pacific Nomad* was the first live-aboard, followed by the *Molly Dean*. Launching *Nai'a* in the early '90s, Rob Barrel ventured into Bligh Water, discovering the now-famous E6 seamount and other sites. Four luxury live-aboards now ply Fijian waters, while dozens of land-based operators have made diving possible in literally all corners of the archipelago.

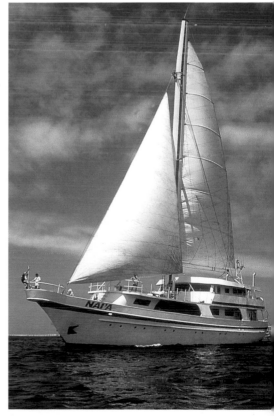

Nai'a is one of several live-aboards based in Fiji.

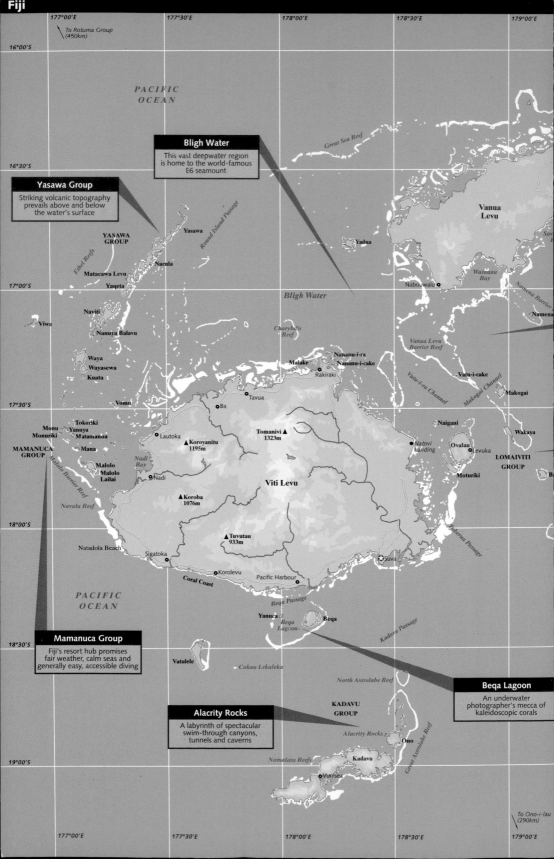

Fiji

To Rotuma Group
(450km)

PACIFIC OCEAN

Bligh Water
This vast deepwater region is home to the world-famous E6 seamount

Yasawa Group
Striking volcanic topography prevails above and below the water's surface

Great Sea Reef

Vanua Levu

YASAWA GROUP

Yasawa

Round Island Passage

Yadua

Savu

Ebal Reefs

Nacula

Matacawa Levu

Yaqeta

Wainunu Bay

Nabouwalu

Namena Barrier

Navití

Bligh Water

Viwa

Nanuya Balavu

Charybdis Reef

Vanua Levu Barrier Reef

Namena

Waya

Wayasewa

Kuata

Nananu-i-ra
Nananu-i-cake

Malake

Rakiraki

Vatu-i-ra Channel

Vatu-i-cake

Makogai Channel

Makogai

Vomo

Tavua

Ba

Naigani

Wakaya

Tomanivi ▲
1323m

Monu
Monuriki

Tokoriki
Yanuya
Matamanoa

Lautoka

▲ Koroyanitu
1195m

Natovi Landing

Ovalau

Levuka

LOMAIVITI GROUP

MAMANUCA GROUP

Mana

Nadi Bay

Viti Levu

Moturiki

Malolo Barrier Reef

Malolo
Malolo Lailai

Nadi

▲ Koroba
1076m

Navala Reef

▲ Tuvutau
933m

Natadola Beach

Sigatoka

Korolevu

Korolevu

Pacific Harbour

Suva

Luberua Passage

Coral Coast

PACIFIC OCEAN

Beqa Passage

Yanuca

Beqa Lagoon

Beqa

Kadavu Passage

Mamanuca Group
Fiji's resort hub promises fair weather, calm seas and generally easy, accessible diving

Vatulele

Cakau Lekaleka

North Astrolabe Reef

KADAVU GROUP

Beqa Lagoon
An underwater photographer's mecca of kaleidoscopic corals

Alacrity Rocks
A labyrinth of spectacular swim-through canyons, tunnels and caverns

Alacrity Rocks

Ono

Great Astrolabe Reef

Namalata Reefs

Kadavu

Vunisea

To Ono-i-lau
(290km)

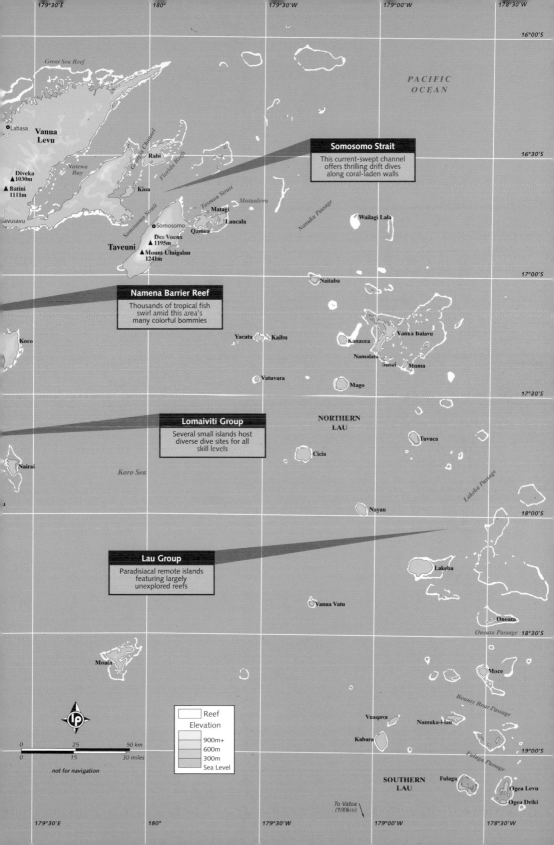

179°30'E   180°   179°30'W   179°00'W   178°30'W

Great Sea Reef

Vanua
Levu

○Labasa

16°00'S

PACIFIC
OCEAN

Natewa Channel

Rabi

▲Diveka
1030m

*Natewa
Bay*

Florida Reefs

16°30'S

▲Batini
1111m

Kioa

avusavu

Tasman Strait

Motualeva

Matagi

Laucala

Somosomo Strait

Qamea

○Somosomo

Taveuni

Des Voeux
▲1195m

▲Mount Uluigalan
1241m

Namuka Passage

●Wailagi Lala

Somosomo Strait
This current-swept channel offers thrilling drift dives along coral-laden walls

17°00'S

Naitaba

Namena Barrier Reef
Thousands of tropical fish swirl amid this area's many colorful bommies

Koro

Yacata   Kaibu

Vanua Balavu

Kanacea

Namalata

Susui Munia

Vatuvara

Mago

17°30'S

Lomaiviti Group
Several small islands host diverse dive sites for all skill levels

NORTHERN
LAU

Tuvuca

Nairai

Koro Sea

Cicia

Lakeba Passage

Nayau

18°00'S

Lau Group
Paradisiacal remote islands featuring largely unexplored reefs

Lakeba

Vanua Vatu

Oneata

Oneata Passage 18°30'S

Moala

Moce

Bounty Boat Passage

Vuaqava   Namuka-i-lau

Kabara

19°00'S

⊕ IP

| 0 | 25 | 50 km |
| 0 | 15 | 30 miles |

not for navigation

	Reef
	Elevation
	900m+
	600m
	300m
	Sea Level

SOUTHERN
LAU

Fulaga

Ogea Levu

Ogea Driki

Fulaga Passage

To Vatoa
(100km)↘

179°30'E   180°   179°30'W   179°00'W   178°30'W

Practicalities

Climate

Fiji has a tropical maritime climate, tempered by the ocean and trade winds. However, due to its steep mountain ranges and the vast area it encompasses, the archipelago can experience a wide range of local conditions, from hot and dry to warm and wet.

The leeward sides of the major islands tend to be dry with clear skies, steady temperatures and ample sunshine. The windward sides are subject to cloudy skies and increased rainfall. Conditions on smaller islands are typically sunny and dry.

The cool, dry months from May to October are considered the best time to visit Fiji, while the hot, wet season generally lasts from December to April.

During the winter months, July to September, divers can expect prime underwater visibility, water temperatures as low as 22°C (72°F) and choppy surface conditions.

In the summer months, November to April, divers will likely find calm seas, but visibility tends to diminish a little as water temperatures rise to 29°C (84°F). This season also experiences an increase in rainfall and the possibility of a cyclone, especially from January to March.

El Niño in Fiji

While Fijian farmers and villagers dread the El Niño global warming phenomenon, which brings drought conditions and water shortages to the country, divers can benefit from the change. Calm seas and lots of sunshine balance cooler than average water temperatures, and lower rainfall translates to excellent visibility.

Language

Fijian, Hindi and English are the archipelago's three main languages. Fijian comprises a multitude of "communalects," all stemming from the Austronesian family of languages. Several consonants will seem unusual to English speakers:

b is pronounced *mb* as in member   g is pronounced *ng* as in sing
c is pronounced *th* as in father   q is pronounced *ng* as in angry
d is pronounced *nd* as in Monday

For example, the city of Nadi is pronounced NAN-di, while the island of Beqa is pronounced BEN-ga.

Say It in Fijian

Some everyday civilities and diving terms will help you win over your Fijian hosts:

Hello	*Bula* (MBU-la)
See you later	*Au sa liu mada*
	(Ow sah liu MAN-da)
Goodbye	*Moce* (MOTH-ey)
Thank you	*Vinaka* (Vee-NAKA)
house	*bure* (MBUR-ey)
boat	*waqa* (WAN-ga)
ocean	*wasawasa*
coral	*lase (LAH-say)*
fish	*ika*
shark	*qio* (ghio)

Suggested reading: *Fijian Phrasebook* published by Lonely Planet

Getting There

Nearly all international flights land at Nadi International Airport, although Air Pacific now offers direct flights between Auckland and Nausori International Airport near Suva. Carriers to Fiji include Air Nauru, Air New Zealand, Air Pacific, Canadian Airlines International, Japan Airlines, Quantas, Polynesian Airlines and Royal Tongan Airlines. Flights are available from Sydney, Melbourne, Auckland, Tokyo, Honolulu, Los Angeles, San Francisco and Vancouver, as well as Pacific island hubs such as Honiara in the Solomons and Port Vila in Vanuatu. Some airlines offer tickets that allow you to hop between Pacific islands for a discounted fare.

Getting Around

Domestic carriers Air Fiji and Sunflower Airlines fly throughout the Fijian islands. Both airlines have strict luggage weight restrictions, allowing only 20kg (44lbs) of free check-in luggage per passenger; there is a fee for additional baggage. Air Fiji (☎ 313 666; www.airfiji.net) is based out of Suva, while Sunflower Airlines (☎ 723 016; www.fiji.to) is based out of Nadi; flights are routed accordingly.

Ferry services also connect many of the larger islands. Ferries have a much more liberal luggage allowance, are inexpensive and allow visitors to mingle with locals. But interisland crossings can be rough and are not always fun on a crowded vessel.

On the larger islands, taxis are a relatively inexpensive way to get around. Local buses are also an option, but if you are traveling with dive gear, it is a very inconvenient way to travel. The buses are often crowded, and luggage stowage is not available. A rental car may be a more expensive mode of travel, but it allows you to travel and explore at your own pace, with ample room for your dive gear. Remember, driving is on the left in Fiji (British style).

Swami Temple marks the south end of Nadi's Main Street.

Gateway City – Nadi

While Suva is Fiji's capital, Nadi (population 31,000) serves as the gateway city, as most international flights arrive at Nadi International Airport, just 9km (5.6 miles) north of the city. There are hotels in all price ranges between the airport and downtown Nadi, and local buses as well as taxis frequent Queens Road, the connecting highway. If you have a reservation at a resort, airport transfers are often included or offered at a reasonable rate.

Downtown Nadi is concentrated around Main Street, which begins just south of the Nadi River bridge and ends at Sri Siva Subramaniya Swami Temple, one of Nadi's most prominent landmarks. Visitors will find most shops and restaurants along Main Street, as well as banks, gas stations and the post office.

Entry

Tourist visas valid for up to four months are granted on arrival to citizens of most countries. The visas may be extended for up to two months, provided you have a valid passport, an onward or return air ticket and adequate funds for your stay. Tourists from excluded countries must apply for visas through a Fijian embassy prior to arrival.

Money

The local currency is the Fiji dollar. Major credit cards are accepted by most hotels, resorts, dive facilities, shops, and travel and rental car agencies. Traveler's checks are also a good option. Automatic teller machines are practically nonexistent.

Be aware that a 10% value-added tax (VAT) is charged on all goods and services; be sure the prices you're quoted include the VAT. Tipping is not encouraged but is appreciated for excellent service.

Time

Fiji lies just west of the international date line. North Americans, for example, will lose a day when traveling to Fiji but gain a day when returning east.

The islands are two hours ahead of Australian Eastern Standard Time, 12 hours ahead of GMT and 20 hours ahead of U.S. Pacific Standard Time. When it's

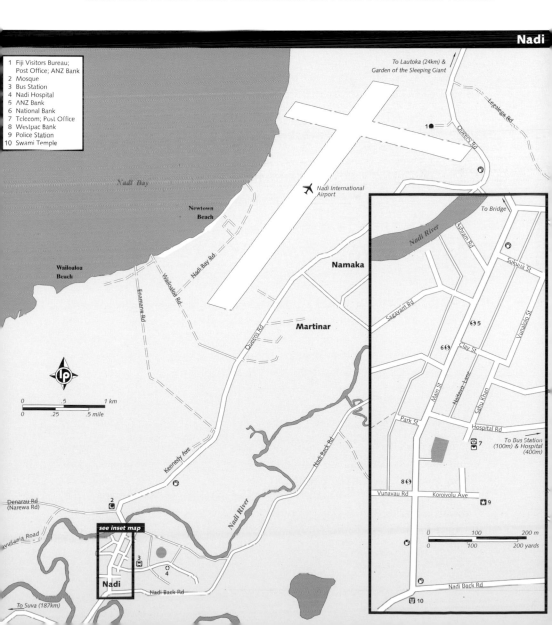

Nadi

1 Fiji Visitors Bureau;
   Post Office; ANZ Bank
2 Mosque
3 Bus Station
4 Nadi Hospital
5 ANZ Bank
6 National Bank
7 Telecom; Post Office
8 Westpac Bank
9 Police Station
10 Swami Temple

noon on Monday in Fiji, it's 10am Monday in Sydney, midnight Sunday in London and 4pm Sunday in San Francisco. Daylight saving time is observed.

Electricity

Electricity throughout Fiji is on a 240V, 50Hz cycle, with three-pin Australian outlets. Some resorts and live-aboards that cater to the U.S. market also have 110V outlets that accept standard two-pronged U.S. plugs, allowing divers and underwater photographers to charge dive light and strobe batteries. If you require 110V outlets for your equipment, inquire with the live-aboard or resort ahead of time.

Bures (thatched huts) set aside for backpackers often have no electricity at all—only gas lamps for reading. Also note that not all resorts have 24-hour electricity. Many resorts that run on generator power turn them off sometime around 10pm and don't turn them back on till 8am or so. Photographers with strobes requiring 12-hour-plus charges should check with their resort.

Weights & Measures

The metric system is standard. In this book, both metric and imperial measurements are given, except for specific references in dive site descriptions, which are given in meters only. Please refer to the conversion chart provided on the inside back cover.

What to Bring
General

Wear lightweight, casual clothing that will protect you from insects and overexposure to the sun. Bathing suits and short shorts for women are practical and acceptable around resorts but should not be worn in public, particularly in or near Fijian villages. A windbreaker is helpful during the rainy season or when the trade winds are blowing. It's a good idea to bring plenty of sunscreen and insect repellent.

Dive-Related

Quality, brand-name rental scuba equipment is available at most dive resorts and operations, though you should inquire ahead of time. Live-aboards typically have only a limited supply of gear for rent, since divers tend to bring their own. During the summer months, a lycra or 3mm suit is all that's required, mostly as protection against sunburn, coral cuts and abrasions. During the winter months, particularly July and August, a 5mm suit is needed to keep warm.

Underwater Photography

Most live-aboards offer onboard E6 processing. *Fiji Aggressor* and *Nai'a* even rent a variety of Nikonos cameras, lenses and strobes. Despite what the brochures may say, most resorts do not offer camera rentals or processing; all too often, they run out of chemicals or the person trained to do E6 is on leave. Be sure to bring all the slide film, videotapes and batteries you need during the trip. Supplies throughout Fiji are very limited and often old or improperly stored.

Business Hours

Most businesses and public markets are open weekdays from 8am to 5pm, and from 8am to 1pm on Saturdays. Souvenir shops in Nadi and Suva stay open until 4pm on Saturdays. Bank hours are 9:30am to 3pm Monday to Thursday, and till 4pm on Fridays. Government offices are open weekdays from 8am to 4:30pm, also till 4pm on Fridays. Many places close for lunch between 1 and 2pm.

Accommodations

Choices range from camping facilities to some of the most exclusive resorts in the world. Keep in mind that Fiji's 10% VAT (value-added tax) is tucked on to all hotel expenses and related services.

Camping without permission is prohibited in Fiji, but there are a few private campgrounds on Viti Levu, Vanua Levu and Taveuni. Guesthouses and backpacker dorms are fairly inexpensive options, and hotels in Nadi and Suva are moderately priced. Resorts in Fiji range from rustic lodges to luxury properties. Most resorts cater to divers, and some offer backpacker rooms for budget travelers.

If money is no object, exclusive resorts include Vatulele Island Resort, Toberua Island Resort, Wakaya Club and Fiji Forbes Laucala Island Resort.

Dining & Food

Restaurants in Fiji typically offer indigenous Fijian, Indian, Chinese or European cuisine. Seafood is on most menus.

Fijian meals include such foods as pork, chicken, fish and native root crops. In a traditional Fijian feast, the food is wrapped in banana leaves, then prepared in a ground oven. The oven, or *lovo*, is a pit lined with stones that are heated by firewood for several hours. The embers are cleared away, and the parcels of food are cooked atop the hot stones. Dessert features puddings made of papaya, banana and *lolo* (coconut cream).

Open markets and roadside stalls offer a range of fresh fruit and vegetables, including traditional roots such as *kumala* (sweet potato), *tavioka* (cassava) and *dalo* (taro), which are typically boiled or baked in a lovo.

Shopping

Duty-free bargains are possible for such items as photographic equipment, VCRs, perfumes, watches, liquor, tobacco and film. But buyer beware: The 10% VAT is levied on most imported items, even if sold in so-called duty-free shops!

Woodcarvings, woven mats, baskets and other handicrafts are readily available throughout Viti Levu, with large shops in Nadi and Suva. The wraparound *sulu*—the national costume for men and women, often in colorful, tropical prints—makes a practical souvenir that you can wear to the beach or when visiting a Fijian village.

Guitarists sport traditional wraparound *sulus*, Fiji's colorful national costume.

When choosing small, useful gifts to bring home, don't overlook Fiji's spices (check your return customs restrictions before buying) such as pepper, ginger, vanilla or cinnamon. Look for attractive gift packages featuring one or several of these spices.

Be sure not to buy any products created from endangered species, such as crafts made from turtle shell. And before buying seashells or trinkets made from shells, consider that most of these animals are killed for their shells. By buying such souvenirs, you will only encourage islanders to collect more live specimens, which in turn can lead to an ecological imbalance on Fiji's reefs.

For instance, the magnificent triton's trumpet is the only predator of the destructive crown-of-thorns sea star. These fleshy, cactus-like echinoderms feed on live coral, and an overpopulation of crown-of-thorns sea stars can lead to the destruction of an entire reef. A healthy triton's trumpet population is necessary to keep their numbers in check.

Activities & Attractions

As Fiji's tourist hub, Viti Levu hosts many of the region's activities and attractions, including a variety of ecotourism and adventure tours and water sports such as whitewater rafting, windsurfing, sailing and surfing, as well as jet-boat excursions.

The outer islands offer more-limited, simpler recreational pursuits. Besides scuba diving and snorkeling, activities in these more remote locations include kayaking, hiking and, of course, beachcombing and simply relaxing on the beach. Visits to native Fijian villages are another popular pastime—just be sure to brush up on Fijian etiquette before you go!

Kayaking

Kayaking is a great way to explore Fiji's shallow reefs, mystical sea caverns and beautiful bays. Most resorts have at least a couple of kayaks available for their guests to venture off-island a bit. On Kadavu you can participate in guided kayak tours ranging from one day to one week, sometimes combined with scuba diving. On Viti Levu visitors can sign up for the **Wainikoroiluva** (Luva for short) **River** inflatable kayak trip, also a guided tour, which takes you through the spectacular Luva River gorge.

Surfing

The best surf is found outside barrier-reef passages, where powerful open-ocean swells break onto the reef. There are plenty of these passages scattered throughout Fiji, but only few of them are accessible. Top spots include **Malolo** and **Wilkes Passages** in the Mamanuca Group (Tavarua and Namotu are home to dedicated surf resorts for this region) and **Frigate Passage** in Beqa Lagoon (Marlin Bay Resort caters to surfers). Winter is surf season, as low-pressure fronts mean high waves, though prime spots have surf year-round.

Horseback Riding

A variety of resorts throughout Fiji offer horseback riding, ranging from short rides on the beach to all-day riding adventures. On Viti Levu, adventure tour agents organize guided multi-day tours that combine activities such as horseback riding, trekking and rafting.

Sailing

Fiji is a sailor's paradise, with pristine cruising areas and various departure points. Since individual villages own most Fijian reefs, it is imperative to seek formal permission before dropping anchor. For details on arrival, departure and customs formalities and general yachting information, contact Yacht Help at ☎ 668 969 (yachthelp@is.com.fj). The Moorings, at Musket Cove Marina on Malolo Lailai, charters yachts for cruising the Mamanuca and Yasawa Groups.

A golden sunset caps a day of South Pacific cruising.

Whitewater Rafting

This unique trek leads you through the barely explored **Upper Navua River** gorge, a deep chasm that slices through Viti Levu's tropical interior. Sometimes referred to as Fiji's Grand Canyon, the gorge is shrouded in a lush rainforest and fed by countless waterfalls. Its challenging rapids make the remote headwaters of the Upper Navua a true adventure.

Jet Boats

Not having any luck spotting sharks? Try the adrenaline-pumping excitement of a jet-boat excursion instead. Incredibly fast and maneuverable, these river rockets blast along the narrow, mangrove-lined corridors of the **Nadi River** at up to 75km/h (45mph). Offered through Shotover Jets Fiji, these 30-minute tours leave from Port Denarau (15km/9 miles south of Nadi International Airport) and can be booked through most hotels and resorts.

Late-Evening Flight? No Problem!

Since U.S.-bound flights generally depart late in the evening, travelers connecting from outer islands often find themselves with several hours to kill before check-in for the international flight.

For many travelers, a good option for their "day in transit" is to simply check into a nearby hotel (such as the Tokatoka, across the street from the airport) and catch some sleep or relax at the pool. If you are feeling more energetic, following are a few ideas to make your last few hours in paradise as enjoyable as possible:

- Visit the **Garden of the Sleeping Giant**. This magnificent orchid collection of the late American actor Raymond Burr is near Lautoka, a half-hour taxi ride north of Nadi.

- Take a taxi down to the **Sheraton Fiji Resort** and spoil yourself with a massage or beauty treatment at the salon. Or enjoy your last Fijian sunset at the resort bar overlooking magnificent Denarau Island Beach.

- Combine a last-minute souvenir-shopping trip to Nadi with a visit to the Hindu **Swami Temple** and a gourmet lunch at **Chefs, the Restaurant**. (Unless you're a vegetarian teetotaler, visit the temple before your meal—visitors are allowed inside the temple, but not if they've consumed alcohol or nonvegetarian food.)

- Take a cruise to the nearby **Mamanuca Group islands**. Tours may include snorkeling, sightseeing, lunch on the beach, sunset cocktails, etc. Often these tours can be booked directly at the airport and include transportation to the vessel.

- Hire a taxi for a one-hour ride to stunning **Natadola Beach**, a great spot to swim, snorkel, surf or sunbathe. Stay for lunch, dinner or cocktails at the intimate Spanish-style bar and restaurant at Natadola Beach Resort.

Useful Tips There is a luggage storage area at the airport, which will make venturing out more convenient. Taxis are very reasonable in Fiji, but you should always negotiate your fare ahead of time. If in doubt, ask at the airport's visitors information office or at any of the nearby hotels for the appropriate fee.

Orchid Island Cultural Center

This cultural center about 7km (4 miles) west of Suva features a replica of a *bure kalou*, a type of ancient Fijian temple once found in every village. Tours include a visit to the chief's house, demonstrations of several Fijian customs and a historical retrospective of cannibalism. All-day tours from Nadi are available.

Garden of the Sleeping Giant

The Sabeto mountain range (or Sleeping Giant Ridge) serves as the backdrop for this orchid farm, a private collection of the late American actor Raymond Burr. Now owned by a Hawaiian corporation, the collection features a dazzling array of magnificent orchid species. The farm is near Lautoka, a scenic half-hour taxi ride from Nadi.

Nature lovers will be drawn to Bouma National Heritage Park on Taveuni.

Hiking

Hiking tours are available to the highlands of Viti Levu, often in combination with a stay in a Fijian village. Around Savusavu on Vanua Levu, hiking excursions through copra plantations and rainforests and to natural hot springs are among the highlights. On Taveuni, **Bouma National Heritage Park** encompasses trails through native rainforest to several cascading waterfalls and natural pools. There is also an eight-hour hike that leads to the mystical mountain lake Tagimaucia, home to a spectacular indigenous flower of the same name.

Village Visits

If you respect local customs and traditions, you'll be welcomed into people's villages and homes, make new friends and forge unforgettable memories. Be sure to dress modestly. A traditional wraparound sulu is usually part of the attire. Women must cover their shoulders and knees. It is impolite to wear shoes into somebody's house, and wearing a hat or touching someone's head is considered an insult.

When visiting a Fijian village, it is customary to present a *sevusevu*, or gift of *yaqona*, the root of the pepper plant *Piper methysticum*. This root is crushed and brewed to make the mildly narcotic drink kava. As you politely ask for permission to visit, present the sevusevu to the *turaga-ni-koro*, the head of the village.

Most resorts and even live-aboards offer visits to Fijian villages. Private excursion companies offer multi-day village visits in the highlands of Viti Levu, as well as combination tours that tie in four-wheel-drive sightseeing trips, backcountry hiking or rafting.

Villagers welcome visitors with a formal kava ceremony.

Diving Health & Safety

SARAH J.H. HUBBARD

General Health

Unlike many tropical dive destinations, Fiji has relatively few health risks or diseases. The potentially fatal mosquito-borne disease malaria, a serious problem in many South Pacific countries, is not a concern here. Occasionally, Fiji experiences outbreaks of dengue fever, another mosquito-borne disease with flu-like symptoms such as fever, headaches and severe joint and muscle pain; there is no prophylactic available. While dengue fever can be dangerous to infants or elderly people, serious complications are rare.

Divers should be especially wary of health hazards such as sun overexposure, diarrhea and infections from coral cuts. These nuisances are easily avoided or minimized by following a few precautions. Be sure to carry waterproof sunblock and lip balm with you and reapply them frequently. When topside, stay in the shade and drink plenty of fluids. Avoid drinking tap water. Bottled water is always a good option, and many resorts also offer flasks of rainwater, which is safe to drink. Wear an exposure suit while snorkeling to avoid sunburn and while diving to avoid coral cuts. If an injury occurs, no matter how small, be sure to clean and treat the wound immediately.

Pre-Trip Preparation

Your general state of health, diving skill level and specific equipment needs are the three most important factors that impact any dive trip. If you honestly assess these before you leave, you'll be well on your way to assuring a successful, safe dive trip.

First, if you're not in shape, start exercising. Second, if you haven't dived for a while (six months is too long), and your skills are rusty, do a local dive with an experienced buddy or take a scuba review course. Finally, inspect your dive gear. Feeling good physically, diving regularly and using reliable equipment will make you a safer diver and enhance your enjoyment underwater.

Diving & Flying

Most divers in Fiji arrive by plane. While it's fine to dive soon *after* flying, it's important to remember that your last dive should be completed at least 12 hours (some experts advise 24 hours, particularly after repetitive dives) *before* your flight home to minimize the risk of decompression sickness, caused by residual nitrogen in the blood.

At least a month before your trip, inspect your dive gear. Remember, your regulator should be serviced annually, whether you've used it or not. If you use a dive computer and can replace the battery yourself, change it before the trip or buy a spare one to take along. Otherwise, send the computer to the manufacturer for a battery replacement.

If possible, find out if the dive center rents or services the type of gear you own. If not, you might want to take spare parts or even spare gear. A spare mask is always a good idea.

Purchase any additional equipment you may need, such as a dive light and tank marker light for night diving, a line reel for wreck diving, etc. Make sure you have at least a whistle attached to your BC. Better yet, add a marker tube.

About a week before taking off, do a final check of your gear, grease o-rings, check batteries and assemble a save-a-dive kit. This kit should at minimum contain extra mask and fin straps, snorkel keeper, mouthpiece, valve cap, zip ties and o-rings. Don't forget to pack a first-aid kit and medications such as decongestants, ear drops, antihistamines and motion sickness tablets.

Signaling Devices

Occasionally a diver becomes lost or is left behind at a dive site—make sure this never happens to you! A diver is extremely difficult to locate in the water, so always dive with a signaling device of some sort, preferably more than one.

One of the best signaling devices and the easiest to carry is a whistle. Even the little ones are extremely effective. Use a zip tie to attach one permanently to your BC. Even better, though more expensive, is a loud air horn that connects to the inflator hose. You simply push a button to let out a blast. It does require air from your tank to function, though.

A great visual device to carry with you is a marker tube, also known as a safety sausage or come-to-me. The best ones are brightly colored and about 3m (10ft) high. These roll up and will easily fit into a BC pocket or clip onto a D-ring. They're inflated orally or with a regulator. Some will allow you to insert a dive light into the tube—a nice feature when it's dark.

A dive light itself is particularly versatile. It can be used during the day for looking into reef crevices and comes in very handy for nighttime signaling. Some feature a special strobe option. Consider carrying at least a small light with you at all times—you might go on an unexpected night dive and be glad to have it.

DAN

Divers Alert Network (DAN) is an international membership association of individuals and organizations sharing a common interest in diving and safety. It includes DAN Southeast Asia and Pacific (DAN SEAP), an autonomous non-profit organization based in Australia. DAN operates a 24-hour diving emergency hot line. DAN SEAP members should call ☎ **61 8 8212 9242**. DAN America members should call ☎ **919-684-8111 or 919-684-4DAN** (-4326). The latter accepts collect calls in a dive emergency.

Though DAN does not directly provide medical care, it does give advice on early treatment, evacuation and hyperbaric treatment of diving-related injuries. Divers should contact DAN as soon as a diving emergency is suspected.

DAN membership is reasonably priced and includes DAN TravelAssist, a benefit that covers medical air evacuation from anywhere in the world for any illness or injury. For a small additional fee, divers can get secondary insurance coverage for decompression illness. For membership questions, contact DAN at ☎ 800-446-2671 in the U.S. or ☎ 919-684-2948 elsewhere. DAN can also be reached at www.diversalertnetwork.org.

Medical & Recompression Facilities

The Fiji Recompression Chamber Facility is in Suva, near the corner of Brewster and Amy streets, just south of the Colonial War Memorial Hospital. There are plans to build a new, private hospital, which will likely incorporate the chamber facilities.

All members of the FDOA (Fiji Dive Operators Association) have been trained how to respond in a diving emergency. They will phone in a chamber alert, and a hyperbaric doctor will assess the situation and arrange transportation to the chamber.

Ideally, your dive operator should phone in the alert, though you may do it yourself by calling ☎ 362 172. Once you've called, however, don't derail the alert procedure or duplicate efforts by calling the facility staff, hospitals or airlines, unless the emergency is critical or life-threatening. Also keep in mind that the chamber is only manned once an alert has been activated—don't call the chamber directly or just turn up at the door, as no one will be there.

Medical Contacts

Fiji Recompression Chamber Facility
Emergency chamber alert (24 hours) ☎ 362 172
Chamber ☎ 305 154
Administration ☎ 850 630; fax: 850 344

Nadi
Nadi Hospital ☎ 701 128
Namaka Medical Center ☎ 722 288

Suva
Colonial War Memorial Hospital ☎ 313 444
Gordon Street Medical Clinic ☎ 313 355/155

Lautoka
Lautoka Hospital ☎ 660 399
Vakabale Street Medical Center ☎ 661 961

Diving in Fiji

Fiji offers divers a wide range of environments, opportunities and challenges. Most of the 74 sites featured in this book are accessible only by boat, in part because of safety concerns. Shallows extend far from most Fijian shorelines, requiring long surface swims to reach diving depths—at low tide, you may even have to walk over the reef flats. Low visibility and longshore currents make it potentially difficult to return to shore.

An increasingly popular option is to dive Fiji's more remote sites from the comfort of a live-aboard. There are four live-aboards based in Fijian waters. The most popular destinations include Bligh Water and the islands of Namena, Wakaya and Gau. Live-aboards also schedule cruises to the Lau Group and even Tonga, as well as exploration cruises. These boats usually travel to sites rarely visited by day charter operators.

Many of Fiji's best sites are in the reef passages between the open ocean and protected lagoons. Some are wide channels featuring several bommies and can be split up over several dives; others are narrow channels easily covered in one heart-pounding dive. As currents in these passages can be quite strong and unpredictable, such sites are more suitable for intermediate or advanced divers and are usually done as drift dives from a support vessel for safety and convenience.

What's a Bommie?

Bommie is the Australian name for an underwater pinnacle and is derived from the aboriginal word *bombora*, meaning dangerous or submerged reef.

Soft corals ball up in still water.

Currents are the lifeblood of the reef, providing nutrients to corals and reef fish and initiating the food chain. When the current is running, fairy basslets and other reef fish dart up from the protective reef into the water column to feed, in turn attracting jacks, trevallies, barracuda and other pelagics looking to snack on the reef fish. At the end of the food chain, sharks patiently patrol the reef, stalking the pelagics.

Please note that most dive site descriptions of soft corals are based on the presence of at least a moderate current, when corals bloom to their fullest extent. When currents are absent, soft corals go limp and curl into tiny balls that can literally disappear into the reef.

Underwater visibility in Fiji is extremely variable and can change within a few hours depending on the tides and direction of the currents (incoming currents

Tips for Drift Diving

Knowing how to deal with currents is an integral part of diving in Fiji. Many operators will allow you to drift dive at current-swept sites—often in channel openings and around offshore pinnacles. A drift dive involves entering the water in one spot and being picked up by the boat wherever you surface. It is an advanced activity that requires the following skills:

- descend without a line and equalize your ears quickly
- manage various degrees of current, including up- and down-currents
- maintain buddy contact
- perform a safety stop without a reference line while maintaining neutral buoyancy

You must be ready to act quickly and decisively on your divemaster and boat driver's instructions. When the driver tells you to get ready, you should don your fins, mask and the rest of your gear. If you wear gloves, it's probably better to carry them in your BC pocket and put them on once underwater. If you wait too long to gear up, you could miss the entry point and drift off the site. Often the driver can reposition the boat for your entry, but if your buddy has already entered and descended, it may be difficult or impossible to reunite. Divers in the water are also at increased risk of injury from the boat's propellers.

Enter the water with little or no air in your BC and descend quickly, taking care to properly equalize your ears and orient yourself to the reef. Get to depth or to the bottom as quickly as you can. Currents are most manageable close to walls and the seafloor. Fighting a current uses up lots of air.

Once down, you can either drift or get behind a rock or ledge just out of the current. The latter is an excellent way to observe sharks, tuna, jacks and barracuda. When you want to move on, simply slip into the current and drift. Follow your dive plan and make sure to perform a safety stop.

End the dive by swimming away from the reef into deeper water, then surface. This will allow the boat driver the time and space to pick you up before the boat drifts onto the reef. Before swimming toward the boat, make sure the driver sees you and gives you the OK to approach. Hand up your camera or dive light to the divemaster, followed by your weight belt.

Some operations will take the rest of your gear from you while you're still in the water, while others will have you climb aboard with your gear on. If you are using a ladder, leave your fins on until you have a firm grip on the rail—they will help you kick to the boat in a current. Fins will also help you kick up over the side of a dinghy.

bring clear seawater into the lagoon; outgoing currents flush cloudy lagoon water back into the sea). Other factors affecting visibility in Fiji include river runoff, seasonal plankton blooms and coral spawning.

Snorkeling

Snorkeling on Fiji's reefs can be a rewarding experience. Protected bays on the resort islands feature clear water, shallow coral gardens and active marine life. For the savvy fish-watching enthusiast, sandy bays and sea grass beds hold special attractions such as pipefish, squid, harlequin shrimp, sea stars, snake eels and other unusual creatures.

Snorkeling near seamounts and reef passages in rich, blue water is a special treat, but requires that you are comfortable swimming in potentially strong currents and choppy seas. Always consult local divemasters before snorkeling at remote offshore locations. As a general rule, do not snorkel alone, and be sure to organize a boat to pick you up if water conditions worsen or any other difficulties arise.

Snorkel the clear waters of Fiji's remote shorelines.

Certification

Many dive operators in Fiji have qualified PADI or NAUI instructors on staff and offer a variety of classes, from Open Water to refresher, advanced and specialty courses. Operators in Nadi and the Mamanuca Group regularly schedule Open Water classes. (The dive shops usually conduct the academic and pool sessions in Nadi and the Open Water dives in the Mamanucas.) The live-aboards *Fiji Aggressor* and *Nai'a* also have onboard instructors who teach Open Water and several other courses.

The cost for Open Water classes varies greatly, depending on the number of students, and some operators have minimum class-size requirements. It's often easier to complete the academic and pool sessions with your local dive shop, then have your shop refer you to an instructor in Fiji for the Open Water dives.

Dive Site Icons

The symbols at the beginning of each dive site description provide a quick summary of some of the important characteristics of each site:

 Good snorkeling or free-diving site.

 Remains or partial remains of a wreck can be seen at this site.

 Sheer wall or drop-off.

 Deep dive. Features of this dive are found in water deeper than 27m (90ft).

 Strong currents may be encountered at this site.

 Strong surge (the horizontal movement of water caused by waves) may be encountered at this site.

 Drift dive. Because of strong currents and/or difficulty in anchoring, a drift dive is recommended at this site.

 Shore dive. This site can be accessed from shore.

 Poor visibility. The site often has visibility of less than 8m (25ft).

 Caves or caverns are prominent features of this site. Only experienced cave divers should explore inner cave areas.

Pisces Rating System for Dives & Divers

The dive sites in this book are rated according to the following diver skill-level rating system. These are not absolute ratings but apply to divers at a particular time, diving at a particular place. For instance, someone unfamiliar with prevailing conditions might be considered a novice diver at one dive area, but an intermediate diver at another, more familiar location.

Novice: A novice diver should be accompanied by an instructor, divemaster or advanced diver on all dives. A novice diver generally fits the following profile:
◆ basic scuba certification from an internationally recognized certifying agency
◆ dives infrequently (less than one trip a year)
◆ logged fewer than 25 total dives
◆ little or no experience diving in similar waters and conditions
◆ dives no deeper than 18m (60ft)

Intermediate: An intermediate diver generally fits the following profile:
◆ may have participated in some form of continuing diver education
◆ logged between 25 and 100 dives
◆ dives no deeper than 40m (130ft)
◆ has been diving in similar waters and conditions within the last six months

Advanced: An advanced diver generally fits the following profile:
◆ advanced certification
◆ has been diving for more than two years and logged over 100 dives
◆ has been diving in similar waters and conditions within the last six months

Regardless of your skill level, you should be in good physical condition and know your limitations. If you are uncertain of your own level of expertise for a particular site, ask the advice of a local dive instructor. He or she is best qualified to assess your abilities based on the site's prevailing dive conditions. Ultimately, however, you must decide if you are capable of making a particular dive, a decision that should take into account your level of training, recent experience and physical condition, as well as the conditions at the site. Remember that conditions can change at any time, even during a dive.

Map Index

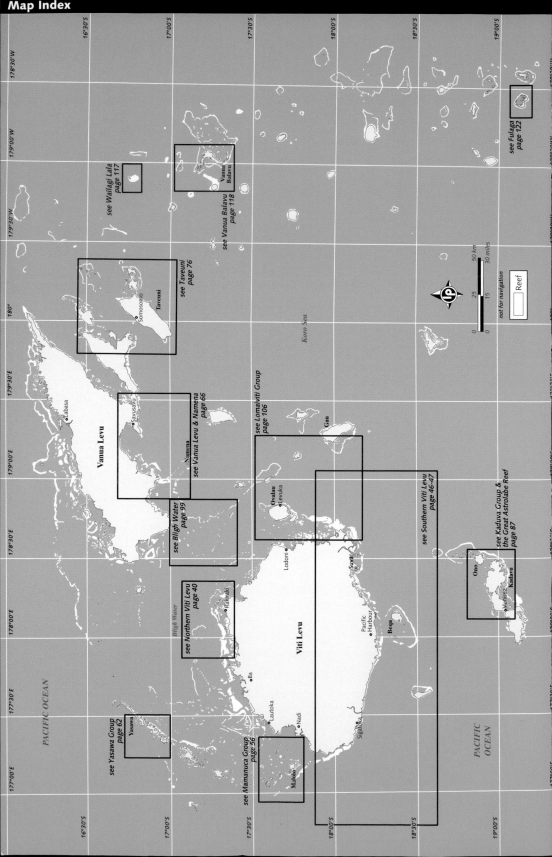

see Yasawa Group
page 62

Yasawa

see Mamanuca Group
page 56

Malolo

PACIFIC OCEAN

Lautoka
Nadi
Sigatoka

Ba

Viti Levu

Pacific
Harbour

Bega

Lodoni

Suva

see Northern Viti Levu
page 40

Rakiraki

Bligh Water

see Bligh Water
page 99

Vanua Levu

Labasa

Savusavu

Namena

see Vanua Levu & Namena
page 66

see Taveuni
page 76

Somosomo

Taveuni

180°

see Wailagi Lala
page 117

see Vanua Balavu
page 118

Vanua
Balavu

see Fulaga
page 122

Koro Sea

Levuka
Ovalau

see Lomaiviti Group
page 106

Gau

see Southern Viti Levu
page 46-47

Ono

Vunisea

Kadavu

see Kaduva Group &
the Great Astrolabe Reef
page 87

PACIFIC
OCEAN

PACIFIC OCEAN

Reef

not for navigation

0   25   50 km
0   15   30 miles

Viti Levu Dive Sites

Spanning some 10,400 sq km (4,000 sq miles), Viti Levu is Fiji's largest island. Seventy-five percent of Fiji's population lives here, and all principal industries and the primary transport and communication systems are also based on the island.

Dominating the interior of the island from north to south is a large mountain range, including Fiji's highest peak, Tomanivi (1,323m/4,340ft). The central highlands lie in the path of the prevailing trade winds, which results in much higher rainfall on the eastern side of the island.

The best dive sites are to the north and south. Dive operators in or close to Nadi, on the western side, usually visit the nearby Mamanuca Group islands.

Most visitors to Fiji arrive in Nadi, on Viti Levu's sunny west coast.

Northern Viti Levu

Diving along the northern shore of Viti Levu is centered on the town of Rakiraki and the nearby offshore islands and reefs. The climate here is similar to that of western Viti Levu—relatively dry with ample sunshine.

Currently, two operators cater to divers at nearby resorts. Ra Divers specializes in a variety of PADI courses, including Open Water and resort courses, while Crystal Divers hosts mostly certified divers. Both operators have explored and discovered their own dive sites and, therefore, generally visit different spots. In calm seas Crystal Divers also ventures to E6, a fantastic dive site located in Bligh Water (see Bligh Water Dive Sites).

Currents tend to be variable at most sites, with the strongest flow occurring between bommies or through narrow canyons.

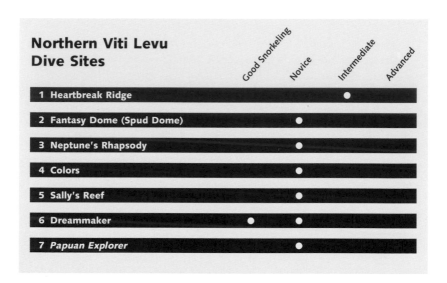

Northern Viti Levu Dive Sites	Good Snorkeling	Novice	Intermediate	Advanced
1 Heartbreak Ridge			●	
2 Fantasy Dome (Spud Dome)		●		
3 Neptune's Rhapsody		●		
4 Colors		●		
5 Sally's Reef		●		
6 Dreammaker	●	●		
7 Papuan Explorer		●		

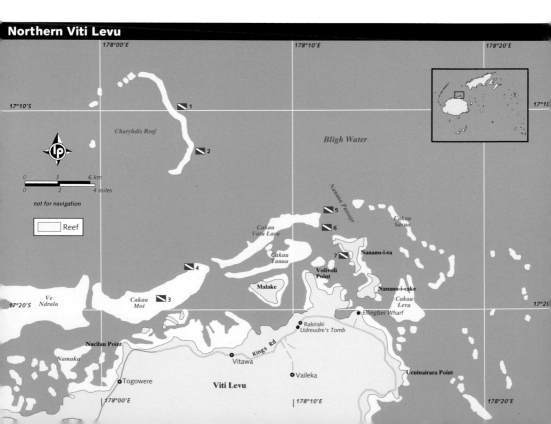

Northern Viti Levu

1   Heartbreak Ridge

When a moderate current is present, this wall dive often provides prime big fish action.

At 20m a ridge extends perpendicular to the reef and wall, gradually sloping down to 27m. Follow this ridge to the point for a chance at spotting schooling barracuda, rainbow runners, walu, grey reef sharks and the occasional silvertip. Friendly batfish, schools of surgeonfish and lots of titan triggerfish are also frequent fly-bys. Other times you may encounter turtles, giant humphead wrasses or schools of bumphead parrot-

Location: Charybdis Reef

Depth Range: 6-27m (20-90ft)

Access: Boat

Expertise Rating: Intermediate

fish. This is one of those spots where you can never tell what you may see!

To finish your dive, head back up the wall and wait out your safety stop at the scenic hard-coral garden in the shallows.

2   Fantasy Dome (Spud Dome)

Also known as Spud Dome, this site comprises three bommies along a reef wall on a sandy sea bottom.

The highlight bommie, which tops out at 10m, is capped by a giant colony of *Pavona clavus* hard coral. From above, the irregular, knobby branches of this reef-building coral look like a pile of potatoes. Here in the shallows you are likely to encounter schooling fusiliers, damselfish and the occasional large flowery cod. At the base of the dome, thousands of garden eels sway in the current.

The other two bommies rise to within 6m of the surface. The sides of both are covered with soft corals, sea fans and patches of sea whips, while one also displays a pretty mosaic of several species of leather coral. Numerous nooks are home to shrimp, spiny lobsters and nocturnal fish. Multihued tropical fish, including coral trout, butterflyfish, lionfish and schools

Location: Charybdis Reef

Depth Range: 6-24m (20-80ft)

Access: Boat

Expertise Rating: Novice

of brilliant basslets, complete the stunning seascape.

Juvenile golden damsels seek shelter among sea fans.

3 Neptune's Rhapsody

A few miles offshore from northern Viti Levu, this site features a large bommie that boasts several tunnels and swim-throughs, all generously lined with sea fans and soft corals. The tunnels are up to 10m long, and each one has several openings. Most of the "windows" frame large soft-coral trees or sea fans reaching

Location: West of Rakiraki

Depth Range: 9-21m (30-70ft)

Access: Boat

Expertise Rating: Novice

up from the seafloor, making for beautiful photo ops. The outside walls of the bommie are inhabited by adhesive anemones, little popcorn shrimp, several large carpet anemones and lots of beautiful angelfish and butterflyfish. Surrounding the bommie is a field of mostly coral rubble, a good environment to spot lizardfish, scorpionfish and dragon wrasses.

Just a short swim from the first bommie, you'll find a second, smaller bommie beside a golden wall, where hundreds of small, golden-yellow soft corals thrive on nutrients brought in by the current funneling between the bommies.

Leave the swim-throughs to find a shimmering golden wall.

4   Colors

Colors is a single, relatively small bommie blanketed with soft corals and sea fans in all imaginable colors and sizes. Throughout the formation you'll come across overhangs and windows literally dripping with dazzling soft corals, making this site an underwater photographer's dream.

Thousands of brilliant basslets swirl in the shallows above the bommie, while large lionfish, numerous sea stars and nudibranchs thrive among the lush coral growth along the sides of the bommie. At about 12m you'll find a carpet anemone that is home to a huge, filter-feeding

Location: Northwest of Rakiraki

Depth Range: 6-18m (20-60ft)

Access: Boat

Expertise Rating: Novice

porcelain crab. A small rock formation next to the bommie is overgrown with dense patches of whip corals, which serve as a stunning photographic backdrop for dozens of golden damselfish.

Thousands of jewel-like basslets swirl atop a living carpet of soft corals.

5   Sally's Reef

Location: North of Nananu-i-ra Island

Depth Range: 6-21m (20-69ft)

Access: Boat

Expertise Rating: Novice

Sally's Reef is dominated by several large bommies that start at about 6m and bottom out at 21m. The coral growth on these bommies is mostly composed of healthy hard corals and a variety of leather coral species. Leather coral is leathery soft but is not as colorful as the *Dendronephthya* soft corals. However, both the leather and soft coral species

belong to the octocoral family, and upon careful observation, you'll notice that each polyp has eight tiny tentacles, giving some of the species a star-like or flower-like appearance.

One of the bommies beside the permanent mooring is laced with undercuts and archways, each densely blanketed with yellow soft corals interspersed with sea fans and whip corals. Amid this lush coral growth, a variety of nudibranchs and cowrie shells make their home. This spot is also well known for encounters with big fish such as humphead wrasses and groupers, as well as eagle rays, reef sharks and walu. A rubble wall slopes down gently behind the bommies and is a good place to spot checkerboard, sixbar and moon wrasses.

6 Dreammaker

At this site, a large underwater pinnacle is riddled with a multitude of canyons, swim-throughs, splits and channels. Generally, the passages are wide enough for a diver to swim through, but some are so densely lined with sea fans and draping soft corals that you must be very careful to avoid doing any damage.

Location: North of Nananu-i-ra Island

Depth Range: 5-21m (15-70ft)

Access: Boat

Expertise Rating: Novice

One particularly spectacular channel boasts numerous overhangs and undercuts, all blanketed with stubby, golden coral trees, bizarre white wire coral and red whip coral. Big spiny puffers and the occasional whitetip reef shark visit the site.

Another channel is sure to catch your eye with its dramatic blend of red sea fans and strawberry-hued soft corals, along with a school of resident red snappers.

The channel floors are a mix of sand and rubble, and if you take the time to slow down and look for small creatures, you'll find an abundance of shrimp gobies, sand perches and triplefins.

7 *Papuan Explorer*

This former cargo ship was purposely sunk in 1990 to create an artificial reef for divers. It lies in water no more than 22m deep about 150m from the jetty at Nananu-i-ra Island. The 33m long wreck sits perfectly upright on its keel, and qualified divers can penetrate the ship.

Coral wreathes the structure, and scores of marine life species, including juvenile sweetlips, juvenile angelfish and puffers, have found shelter within the wreck. Divers have fed many of the fish here, so expect a warm welcome from

Location: Nananu-i-ra Island

Depth Range: 16-22m (53-73ft)

Access: Shore

Expertise Rating: Novice

schools of batfish, unicornfish, butterflyfish and sweetlips. Lionfish, turtles and stingrays are also common visitors to the area.

The passages at Dreammaker pinnacle are blanketed in delicate soft corals and sea fans.

Southern Viti Levu

For the purpose of scuba diving, southern Viti Levu comprises Navula Reef, the Coral Coast (home to many resorts), Vatulele, Beqa Lagoon and Toberua Passage.

The Coral Coast, reaching from Natadola Beach to the village of Naboutini, is generally influenced by the sunny and dry weather pattern of western Viti Levu, while areas east of Pacific Harbour are susceptible to more rainfall. However, the popular resort islands Toberua, Beqa and Vatulele are far enough offshore that they are considered to be outside the mainland's rain belt. Some of Viti Levu's top sites are within the 360 sq km (140 sq mile) Beqa Lagoon and along its 64km (40 mile) long barrier reef.

Fruit stands line Queen's Road.

Vatulele Island is 32km (20 miles) south of Korolevu, off the southern coast of Viti Levu. A mostly flat, yet stunning island with lovely white-sand beaches and dense vegetation, Vatulele serves as the base for one of Fiji's most exclusive resorts.

Several dive operators based out of Pacific Harbour, Suva and the Coral Coast run regular charters to Beqa, Vatulele and other small offshore islands and pinnacles. Marlin Bay Resort, on Beqa, covers all Beqa Lagoon sites. Most dive sites off the southern coast of Viti

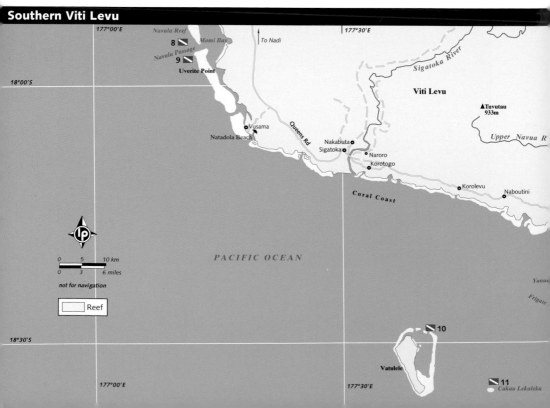

Southern Viti Levu

Levu consist of bommies covered in soft corals and sloping walls populated by pelagics and an abundance of invertebrates and small tropical fish. Visibility varies with currents and rainfall runoff from the main island.

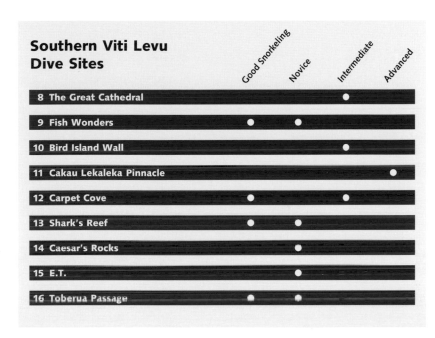

Southern Viti Levu Dive Sites	Good Snorkeling	Novice	Intermediate	Advanced
8 The Great Cathedral			●	
9 Fish Wonders	●	●		
10 Bird Island Wall			●	
11 Cakau Lekaleka Pinnacle				●
12 Carpet Cove	●		●	
13 Shark's Reef	●	●		
14 Caesar's Rocks		●		
15 E.T.		●		
16 Toberua Passage	●	●		

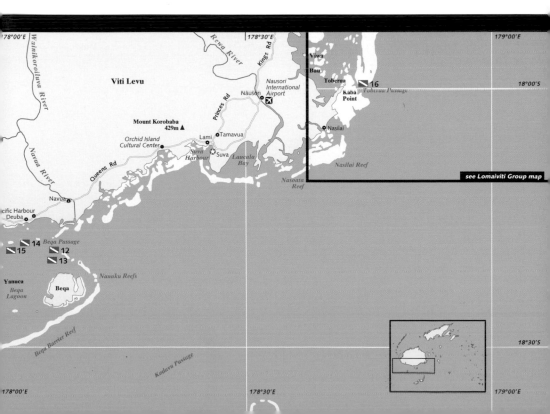

8 The Great Cathedral

Recently discovered by dive shop Scuba Bula, this large site with varied topography is known for good visibility and fantastic hard corals. On the outer edge of the southern reef, the site is ideally approached as a drift dive during an incoming tide.

Location: Navula Reef

Depth Range: 6-27m (20-87ft)

Access: Boat

Expertise Rating: Intermediate

At the beginning of the dive, you'll drop down to a huge overhang that cuts back sharply into the sheer wall—one of the few spots on the dive to see soft coral and whip coral in abundance. Tawny nurse sharks and turtles frequent the underside of the overhang.

As you progress along the wall, the topography changes to a more gradual slope, allowing beautiful gardens of staghorn and cabbage coral to thrive. Just off the slope are several coral plateaus boasting gigantic yet very fragile table and plate corals. One of the coral plateaus features a great swim-through that cradles several resident spiny lobsters and a semi-resident nurse shark.

Other marine life you may observe includes schools of blue-and-yellow fusiliers, several large batfish and whitetip reef sharks, along with several colorful butterflyfish and wrasses.

9 Fish Wonders

On the south side of Navula Passage, Fish Wonders is ideal for first-time divers, provided there is no current.

You'll first drop down about 5m onto a large shelf known as the Fish Wonders

Location: Navula Reef

Depth Range: 5-22m (15-70ft)

Access: Boat

Expertise Rating: Novice

Shoals of yellowfin goatfish will greet you.

Plateau. Shoals of yellowfin goatfish and bluestripe snappers will be there to greet you. There is even a resident stonefish, nicknamed "Grunge."

Descend to between 10 and 12m and you'll reach a sand floor dotted with numerous scattered coral heads. Keep an eye out for stingrays, moray eels, lionfish and dozing whitetip reef sharks. One shark in particular has been known to approach within a few meters of students and watch as they practice Open Water training skills. Also look for a large anchor of unknown origin.

When the current is running, this site is considered more of an advanced dive, and the approach to it changes. With an incoming current, you start the dive in the passage, home to one of the most prolific soft-coral walls in western Fiji, along with lots of grey reef sharks and schools of up to 15 eagle rays. Go with the flow and you'll end up drifting around the corner to Fish Wonders Plateau. Watch for the stonefish during your safety stop.

10   Bird Island Wall

Bird is a tiny island, basically comprising a heap of jagged rocks that serves as a nesting ground for hundreds of Fijian seagulls.

Location: Northeast of Vatulele Island

Depth Range: 12-40m+ (40-130ft+)

Access: Boat

Expertise Rating: Intermediate

The island's barrier reef features a sheer wall that drops straight down to 30m, where it meets a white-sand bottom gently sloping down into the abyss. The white sand reflects the sunlight, coloring the clear water a rich, azure blue. This is an ideal spot to observe razor wrasses, garden eels, ghost crabs and deep-water urchins.

reported on occasion. In addition, this is an excellent site to spot a number of moray eels.

Soft coral is sparse along the sheer wall, but you'll discover nice patches of hard-coral growth and several overhangs blessed with scarlet bouquets of whip coral. Vividly patterned angelfish and butterflyfish are plentiful, but the site's dive highlights usually involve encounters with large marine life. There are several resident loggerhead turtles, manta rays and hammerhead sharks. Swim-bys of walu, tuna and jacks are also frequent, while marlin sightings are

Butterflyfish share Bird Island's reef with bigger critters.

11 Cakau Lekaleka Pinnacle

Cakau Lekaleka Pinnacle, or The Pinnacle for short, is in exposed open water. There are no barrier reefs or nearby islands to offer protection from wind and large swells, so diving at this spectacular site is only possible when weather conditions allow. Accordingly, the site is only suitable for very experienced divers.

Location: Between Vatulele Island and Beqa Lagoon

Depth Range: 24-40m+ (80-130ft+)

Access: Boat

Expertise Rating: Advanced

This submerged seamount is about 800m in diameter and is deeply undercut, lending the seamount a mushroom-like shape. At low tide, the top of the pinnacle actually breaks the surface, but due to its contour, divers usually descend straight to 24m, where the huge undercut levels out a bit.

The Pinnacle is considered one of Fiji's top dive sites for pelagic encounters. While the current is generally robust enough to trigger the food chain, the flow is often quite manageable for divers. As you drift along the wall, don't over-look the blue water, where you're most likely to spot creatures such as brilliant mahimahi, stout eagle rays, schooling hammerheads, nurse sharks, the occasional tiger shark and lots of grey reef sharks. You'll also see shoals of butterfly-fish, surgeonfish and other tropicals, though coral growth is quite sparse.

12 Carpet Cove

Named for the multitude of carpet anemones found in the shallows, this spot is also known as Yanuca Shallows and Seven Sisters, presumably after the many bommies at the site. Besides offering an excellent reef dive, this site also features a wreck.

Location: Beqa Lagoon

Depth Range: 6-30m (20-100ft)

Access: Boat

Expertise Rating: Intermediate

A Japanese fishing boat was purposely scuttled here in 1994 as an artificial reef. The wreck sits upright in the sand—the deepest section at 30m, the shallowest at 21m. Soft coral has established itself along the railings and portholes, while sponges have encrusted plates along the steel hull. There are surprisingly few fish on the wreck, but with such a beautiful reef nearby, that is quite understandable.

From the wreck, a rubble wall slopes gently up to 6m. Look for the magnifi- cent, bright blue ribbon eels at a depth of 18 to 20m—you may even spot two in one hole. Also be on the lookout for leaf scorpionfish and large lionfish. Scattered bommies add colorful splashes to a sea-scape that becomes more dense and spectacular as you ascend. Groups of small hard-coral structures and carpet anemones are flanked by multihued soft corals, and brilliant red sea fans are often lavishly decorated with yellow, red or orange crinoids and accompanying soft corals. With such classic wide-angle setups, Beqa Lagoon draws many underwater photographers.

An intact wreck and a lush, dazzling reef await divers and photographers at Carpet Cove.

Open Wide Underwater

Shooting wide-angle images on Fiji's colorful reefs can be both extremely challenging and rewarding. Challenging when you are dealing with currents, contrasty light conditions and extreme color variations. Rewarding when you succeed in capturing the profusion of colors and shapes the coral gardens and masses of brilliant tropical fish display.

To succeed, you should read up on the subject, take classes and practice a lot. Here are a few tips to get you started:

First, it is important that you learn to identify colors underwater. All of us learned in our Open Water class that colors are absorbed by water at depth. We frequently see underwater photographers miss out on gorgeous wide-angle shots as they obliviously swim past stunning photo opportunities of crimson reds, orange, pinks and purples because they appear a boring gray, brown or black. If necessary, use a light to identify the colors.

Next, you'll have to learn how to deal with currents. Some of Fiji's most active and brilliant wide-angle settings are where the current is the strongest. There is little chance to shoot a great image when you are exhausting yourself in a current or struggling to keep your strobes in place. Your best bet is to choose a spot where you can get out of the current, dig yourself into the rubble or latch onto a rock or piece of dead coral. As beautiful as a pristine reef is, underwater photographers sometimes prefer areas with some damage and rubble, as grabbing hold tends to be the only way to get close to the reef without causing damage yourself.

Next, you have to illuminate the scene and balance the light. We recommend using two strobes, each aimed at the specific subjects they are to light up. If one side of your frame is dominated by pink sea fans, while the other side features purple soft coral, you'll have to adjust your strobes accordingly. As the light-colored sea fan will reflect more light, adjust that strobe to half or quarter power to avoid overexposure. The darker soft coral will absorb light, so you probably have to shoot full power, depending on your depth, etc. Of course, you will want to bracket both your exposures and strobe settings.

If you want to include the sun in your image or capture basslets swarming in and out of the coral, you'll need to set a shutter speed of at least 1/125 of a second.

As far as equipment is concerned, images of equal quality are possible with both housed cameras using an 18 or 20mm lens and Nikonos V cameras fitted with a 15mm lens. Most underwater photographers choose their camera setup based on personal preference and budget.

13   Shark's Reef

Home to several whitetip reef sharks, Shark's Reef is a great site for new divers or simply for a shallow second dive.

Location: Beqa Lagoon

Depth Range: 5-15m (15-50ft)

Access: Boat

Expertise Rating: Novice

Several small bommies sit in a circle, close enough together that it's possible to see them all in one dive. The current-exposed sides of each bommie are sharply undercut and lavishly adorned with gorgonian sea fans, black coral trees and soft corals.

This site is also an excellent fish-watching spot. The long, iridescent trumpetfish are passive here and allow divers to get very close. Also look for large lionfish and huge scrawled filefish, as well as dragon wrasses and other juvenile wrasses along the rubble bottom surrounding the bommies. Among the leather coral atop the bommies is an abundance of Moorish idols, striking teardrop butterflyfish and regal angelfish.

A lone trumpetfish tries to blend in among sea fans.

14   Caesar's Rocks

This site first got noticed when the U.S. magazine *Skin Diver* trumpeted it as the "Mecca of Pacific Diving." It's still an excellent site, though many other world-class sites have since been discovered throughout Fiji.

Location: Beqa Lagoon

Depth Range: 6-18m (20-60ft)

Access: Boat

Expertise Rating: Novice

Caesar's Rocks consists of 10 bommies, all beautifully honeycombed with tunnels, windows and caves and generously adorned with a kaleidoscope of soft corals. Amid this wealth of color, look for tiny critters such as blennies, brittle stars and a variety of nudibranchs.

A highlight of the dive is the huge tunnel that cuts through one of the rocks at a depth of 15m. The inside wall and tunnel openings are lined with encrusting sponges, huge gorgonian sea fans and black coral trees. The tunnel is also home to the striking longnose hawkfish. Keep an eye out for schools of batfish, as well as walu, tuna, turtles and the occasional manta ray.

15 E.T.

The highlight of this dive is a huge tunnel more than 30m long and 5m in diameter that splits twice into additional tunnels and chambers. At a depth of 30m, the tunnel cuts all the way through a large bommie. The sides of the tunnel are lined with sea fans, soft corals and the unusual, thin-stalked *Siphonogorgia*

Location: Beqa Lagoon

Depth Range: 9-21m (30-70ft)

Access: Boat

Expertise Rating: Novice

Bring a light to appreciate this colorful, coral-lined tunnel.

coral. The ceiling is densely encrusted with orange tubastrea cup corals, and both openings boast lush coral growth, making for phenomenal photo ops.

Glide through the tunnel to reach an opening that leads to a second-story tunnel and then a short, third-story tunnel about halfway through. Both upper tunnels are packed with soldierfish, while the openings are blanketed with coral growth. Take a light on this dive to bring out some of the fantastic color lying hidden in the darkness.

Along the bommie wall outside the tunnel, you're likely to encounter several of the large resident lionfish, some tiny but vibrant nudibranchs, flatworms and two ribbon eels that make their home at the tunnel's main opening.

Fireproof Fijians

Fijian legend tells of a warrior from the Sawau tribe who once captured a spirit god, and in exchange for his life, the spirit gave the warrior and all his descendants the power over fire.

To this day, members of the Sawau tribe on Beqa Island are able to walk on white-hot stones without getting burned. The performance is deeply steeped in tradition and requires that the chosen men avoid women and the consumption of coconut. In a wide round pit dug for the ceremony, large stones are placed and topped with a huge log fire that will burn and heat the stones for many hours. The logs are then removed and the stones leveled before the event begins. The fire walkers then enter the pit and slowly walk barefoot on the white-hot stones, followed by a group that moves to the hottest part of the pit and chants a song. None of the performers appears to suffer any harm from the heat.

Tourists can catch firewalking shows on Beqa Island, organized by Marlin Bay Resort, or at Pacific Harbour.

BILL KRITZBERG

16   Toberua Passage

Toberua Passage marks where the barrier reef breaks up into a series of channels and outcrops.

The array of walls and canyons can be split up over several dives, most offering good snorkeling conditions. The shallow reeftops boast pristine hard-coral gardens, and the many overhangs are good spots to look for shrimp, crabs and other invertebrates. Turtles and sea snakes frequent the passage, and from time to time, sharks wander through. Reef fish are abundant and include colorful butterflyfish, angelfish and wrasses.

Toberua Passage is suitable for all experience levels and is generally so calm that glass-bottomed boats offer tours.

Location: Toberua Passage

Depth Range: 5-15m (15-50ft)

Access: Boat

Expertise Rating: Novice

Admire banded sea snakes from a distance.

Mamanuca Group Dive Sites

Consisting of about 20 mostly beach-rimmed isles, the Mamanuca Group is just off Viti Levu's west coast. Due to the islands' proximity to Nadi and Lautoka, and their generally dry and sunny weather, the Mamanucas host many of Fiji's most popular tourist resorts. The majority of the resorts are reachable via a 30- to 90-minute boat ride or a short, scenic flight from Nadi.

These islands offer sunny skies and many resorts.

Diving generally takes place on or near Malolo Barrier Reef, with sites throughout the island chain. There is also a marine sanctuary encompassing the reefs around Beachcomber and Treasure islands. Dive sites in the Mamanucas are quite varied in regard to underwater terrain—including channels, walls and bommies—and for the most part, diving in this protected island chain is quite easy. You

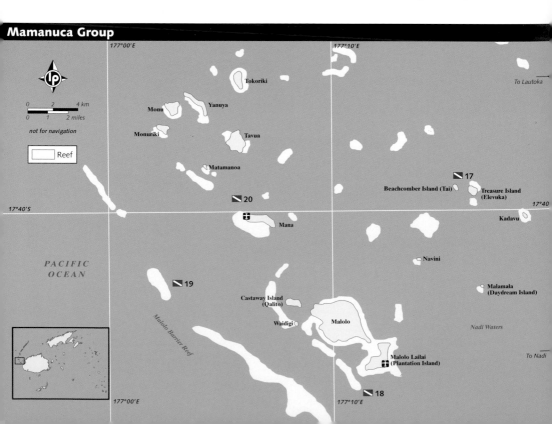

Mamanuca Group

rarely have to be concerned about heavy ocean swells, wind chop, strong currents or long boat rides. Expect to see a wide assortment of hard and soft corals as well as an abundance of friendly, often hand-fed fish.

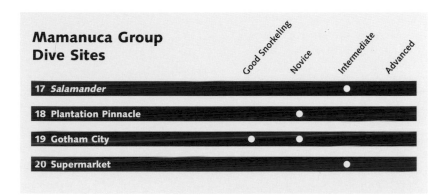

Mamanuca Group Dive Sites	Good Snorkeling	Novice	Intermediate	Advanced
17 Salamander				●
18 Plantation Pinnacle			●	
19 Gotham City		●	●	
20 Supermarket				●

17 Salamander

When this former Blue Lagoon Cruises ship was decommissioned, several dive operators got together and bought it to create an artificial reef. The vessel was stripped, its pipes and bolts removed, and then sunk in 1994. The 36m wreck sits upright on a rubble seafloor.

Over the years, a variety of soft corals and anemones have established themselves on the wreck and continue to flourish. Clouds of silver sweepers inhabit the cabins, while a friendly giant puffer makes his home on the aft deck. Macrophotographers will be pleased to find a variety of nudibranchs, cleaner shrimp, popcorn shrimp and gobies. For qualified divers, limited penetration into the bridge and some of the cabins is possible.

Despite the depth, the wreck also makes for a popular night dive due to

Location: Near Treasure and Beachcomber Islands

Depth Range: 21-28m (70-90ft)

Access: Boat

Expertise Rating: Intermediate

plentiful marine life that includes sleeping parrotfish and prowling octopuses.

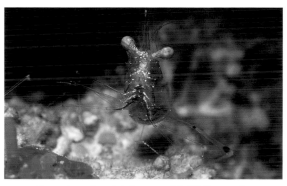

Several species of shrimp now inhabit the wreck.

18 Plantation Pinnacle

This drift dive starts on a pinnacle that tops out 6m from the surface. The peak is exquisitely adorned with bubble-tip and magnificent anemones, as well as healthy patches of leather corals and soft corals.

Location: South of Malolo Lailai Island

Depth Range: 6-23m (20-75ft)

Access: Boat

Expertise Rating: Novice

Drop down to 12m on the current-exposed northern side to find a large undercut with several nooks and crannies and a window that is densely overgrown with an unusual peach-colored soft coral and blood-red sponges. Within this formation, look for friendly squirrelfish, cleaner shrimp and little red-and-white pipefish.

Glide down the pinnacle from here and you'll eventually come to a large tunnel, 3m in diameter and at least 15m long, that cuts through the entire pinnacle. Inside the tunnel, yellow soft-coral trees carpet the ceiling and walls. At one end of the tunnel you'll see a row of large black-coral trees inhabited by longnose hawkfish.

Once you leave the tunnel, explore the pinnacle and you may spot one of the resident stonefish. Or, find the line secured close to one end of the tunnel and follow it south to a second pinnacle. The sides of this pinnacle are more barren, except for numerous wire corals that provide shelter for tiny gobies and shrimp. Atop the peak is a soft-coral garden interspersed with anemones, pipefish, leaf scorpionfish and arceye, dwarf and blackside hawkfish.

You'll find an unusual peach-colored soft coral at this site.

19 Gotham City

Gotham City is inside the barrier reef lagoon, near one of the smaller passages. Thus, the site is flushed with plenty of nutrients, yet water conditions tend to be quite favorable.

Location: West Malolo Barrier Reef

Depth Range: 6-23m (20-75ft)

Access: Boat

Expertise Rating: Novice

Two bommies comprise a formation resembling the humps of a camel. As you descend to the first hump, where a permanent mooring is set up, you'll find yourself surrounded by lots of friendly fish. (Watch your step, as two stonefish have recently set up residence at the base of the mooring!) Fish here are used to being fed, and species such as sergeant majors, butterflyfish, batfish and triggerfish will not hesitate to approach divers. On occasion this includes a couple of titan triggerfish, which sport sets of horrendous teeth.

Gotham City first drew its name from the many huge batfish that resided at the site and often approached divers. Sadly, spearfishers took many of them, though the surviving juveniles are now a good size and getting just as friendly.

Along the slopes of both pinnacles, expect to find hard and soft corals, schooling goatfish and bluestripe snappers, and several humphead wrasses. This is also a good place to find flatworms and a variety of colorful nudibranchs.

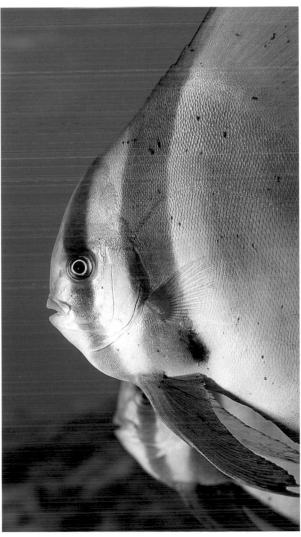

Huge, friendly batfish gave Gotham City its name.

20 Supermarket

Just north of Mana Island, Supermarket has become one of Fiji's best-known dive sites, and it is certainly one of the most thrilling.

Over many years, Mana Island's living legend "Sharkman," Apisai Bati, has gained the confidence and respect of reef sharks and is now able to hand-feed them. Twice weekly, on Thursdays and Sundays, the sharks are fed, and divers are invited to observe and photograph the spectacle.

Many whitetips, some greys and a few blacktips have shown up at the feedings. While an average of 10 sharks attends each meal, as many as 30 have turned up, but rarely fewer than 5. The feeding usually takes about 10 minutes, then divers move on to enjoy the rest of the dive site, although the sharks remain nearby

Location: Mana Island

Depth Range: 6-30m (20-98ft)

Access: Boat

Expertise Rating: Intermediate

and are frequently sighted throughout the dive.

For many divers the sharks are Supermarket's prime draw, but sharks or no sharks, this is a great site. The shallow plateau where the feedings are organized consists of a rock and rubble bottom with numerous scattered coral heads. An abundance of friendly raccoon, saddleback, pennant and other butterflyfish readily approach divers

Feeding the Frenzy

A shark feed can be both exhilarating and educational. While the feedings at Supermarket are controlled and well-organized, there are downsides to these staged performances:

Danger Sharks are wild animals, and as such, they are generally unpredictable. As the number of organized shark feedings increases, so too does the potential for injury to participating divers.

Unnatural Acts Feeding the same territorial animals time and again may condition sharks to lose their wariness of humans (and vice versa). Sharks that grow dependent on these "free lunches" may unlearn vital survival skills. Some have developed Pavlovian responses to the sound of revving boat motors.

Reef Damage As the number of visitors to these shark feedings increases, the potential for site destruction is compounded.

Ultimately, divers must decide for themselves, weighing the downsides against the thrill of the experience. Of course, in Fiji there are plenty of opportunities for natural open-water encounters with these awesome predators.

and are fun to photograph. From here the wall drops sharply, and you can follow it in either direction. Although this dive is generally planned as an anchor dive, some operators organize it as a drift dive so you can just ride the current and not worry about beating it back to the boat.

Along the wall you'll find coral gardens flush with both soft and hard corals and a number of patrolling sharks—even on days the sharks haven't been fed.

Take time to browse Supermarket, which features a healthy reef and hungry sharks.

Yasawa Group Dive Sites

A chain of some 20 ancient volcanic islands, the Yasawa Group extends for 90km (60 miles) in an almost straight line. The mostly hilly and somewhat rugged islands are well known for their sun-drenched white beaches and spectacular, crystal-clear lagoons. There are a few upmarket as well as budget resorts on the islands, but transportation remains a bit of a problem. Traveling by boat takes a long time and can be risky if the weather turns, since there is a lot of open ocean to cross. The

Yasawa Group

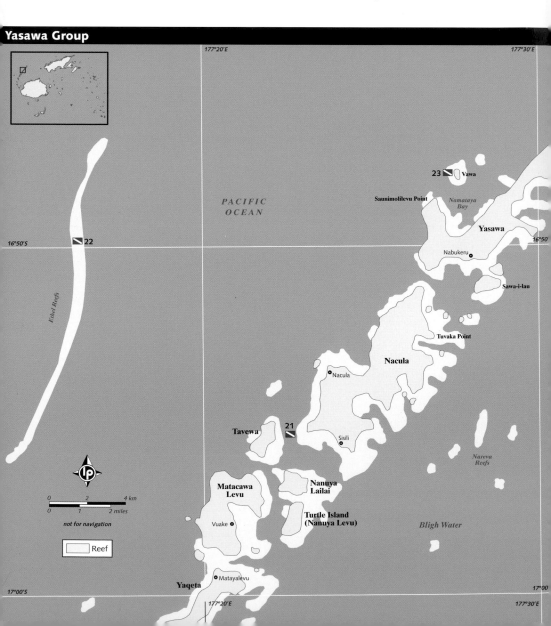

upmarket resorts have their own planes, but luggage weight is normally restricted to 15kg (35lbs).

Most resorts offer diving, and the local sites are recognized for water clarity, brilliant corals and pristine reefs.

Healthy, current-swept reefs attract big fish like these schooling barracuda at The Zoo.

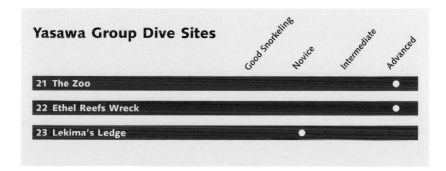

Yasawa Group Dive Sites	Good Snorkeling	Novice	Intermediate	Advanced
21 The Zoo				●
22 Ethel Reefs Wreck				●
23 Lekima's Ledge			●	

21 The Zoo

Between Tavewa and Nacula Islands, this site features a steep, current-flushed wall that is a natural lure for big fish.

Location: East of Tavewa Island

Depth Range: 8-40m+ (27-130ft+)

Access: Boat

Expertise Rating: Advanced

You are likely to encounter schools of barracuda, walu, Spanish mackerel and trevallies. Blacktip and whitetip sharks are also common—some quite large. Carved with numerous overhangs, the wall is clustered with sea fans and soft coral, while the reeftop delights with a beautiful hard-coral garden. Be sure to check the overhangs for schooling soldierfish, longjaw squirrelfish, cleaner shrimp and spiny lobsters. You are also likely to see many large and colorful coral trout darting about the overhangs and coral formations.

Bluefin trevallies can reach 1m (3ft) in length.

Sandy patches gently slope down from several breaks in the sheer wall. These slides are great spots to slow down and search for elegant and fire dartfish (and Helfrich's dartfish at the 40m level), triplefins, shrimp gobies and mantis shrimp.

Due to the depth and possibility of strong currents, this dive is only recommended for experienced divers.

22 Ethel Reefs Wreck

This large steamship (circa early 18th century) probably foundered around 1910—though any details, including the ship's name, remain a mystery. Although the hull is no longer intact, it makes for a great dive.

Location: Ethel Reefs

Depth Range: 5-15m (15-50ft)

Access: Boat

Expertise Rating: Advanced

Resting on a flattop reef that drops off to the west and east, the wreck is quite exposed to currents and surge. Consequently, the debris field offers excellent shelter to a variety of fish and critters. An abundance of spotted sweetlips, along with several moray eels, pufferfish and rays, have taken up residence amid the scattered wreckage, which includes the steam engine, condensers, several anchors, a windlass and the 30m long propeller shaft. Look closely to find pipefish, nudibranchs, shrimp and several species of cardinalfish among the artifacts.

Several moray eels, including this giant moray, have made their homes amid the wreckage.

23 Lekima's Ledge

This exciting and dramatic dive is on the leeward side of the small volcanic island Vawa. The ancient lava cliff formations that shape the island continue underwater and offer a superb backdrop for an array of soft corals.

Generally, your dive starts at the foot of the west-facing cliffs, and you ride the current nearly 1km around the ledge to the south side of the island. The underwater scenery is striking, with a series of ridges and fingers reaching from 22 to 5m. A ledge at 5m makes a perfect safety stop.

This is a great spot to observe schools of convict tangs and other members of the surgeonfish family, as well as the small, distinctly marked leopard wrasse. If you are lucky, you may also encounter a school of the odd-looking bumphead parrotfish.

Location: Vawa Island

Depth Range: 5-23m (15-75ft)

Access: Boat

Expertise Rating: Novice

Where the volcanic rocks break the surface, waves often pound against the cliffs, creating bubbly "thunderclouds." This phenomenon has earned the site the nickname "Riders on the Storm." While novice divers generally stay deep enough to remain in calm water, experienced divers often venture up to play with the thunderclouds toward the end of the dive, allowing the surge to carry them through shallow canyons near the cliff.

Vanua Levu & Namena Dive Sites

Vanua Levu

With a population of approximately 130,000, Vanua Levu is Fiji's second-largest island. Savusavu is the island's tourist hub, consisting of two straight rows of shops, a couple of banks and the post office, all along one main road, lending the town a frontier-like look. The terrain surrounding Savusavu is marked by palm-covered rolling hills, white-sand beaches and amazingly colorful sunsets—perhaps explaining the presence of several luxurious and

Savusavu is Vanua Levu's diving and tourist hub.

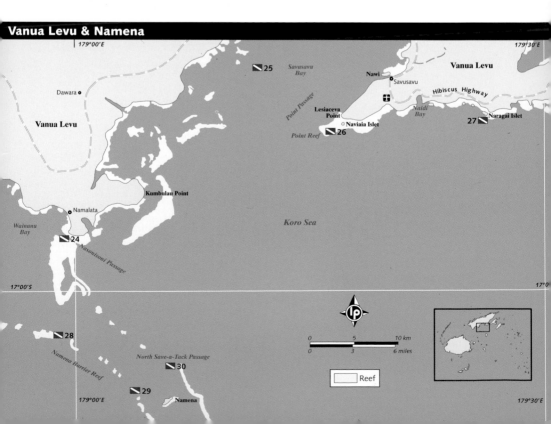

tastefully designed resorts. Most of these resorts are situated east of Savusavu along the southern stretch of the Hibiscus Highway.

The diving along Vanua Levu's southern coast boasts interesting seascapes, with coral-covered bommies and a great variety of reef fish and macro critters. Some of the operators on Vanua Levu will also organize day charter tours to Namena and the Somosomo Strait (see Taveuni Dive Sites).

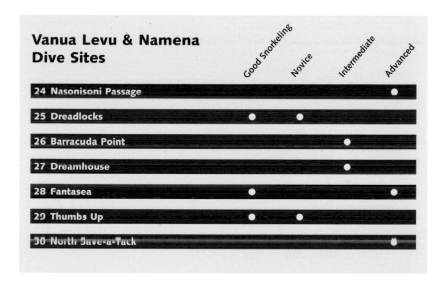

Vanua Levu & Namena Dive Sites	Good Snorkeling	Novice	Intermediate	Advanced
24 Nasonisoni Passage				●
25 Dreadlocks		●	●	
26 Barracuda Point				●
27 Dreamhouse				●
28 Fantasea		●		●
29 Thumbs Up		●	●	
30 North Save-a-Tack				●

24 Nasonisoni Passage

This is a spectacular drift dive in a nearly 2km long passage that cuts through a large reef formation just southeast of Wainunu Bay.

The passage can be split up over two dives. The south side features a string of small, coral-embellished bommies that host lots of colorful marine life, as well as a few whitetips and other pelagics. However, Nasonisoni's most popular dive is along the north wall, which spans the passage.

The wall drops to about 20m, slopes gently to 30m, then drops sharply again. The sloped area between 20 and 30m is where you want to be when, about 15 to 20 minutes into your dive, you feel the current pick up and your "flight" begins.

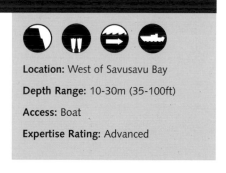

Location: West of Savusavu Bay

Depth Range: 10-30m (35-100ft)

Access: Boat

Expertise Rating: Advanced

(Don't be shy about spreading you arms like a bird—it's fun!) A huge field of purple soft-coral trees dominates the wall and plunges from 20m to well below the recreational dive limit.

Along the way you may see sharks, barracuda or jacks, but there is no stopping. The current is usually far too strong, and you're just along for the ride. At end of the passage, hook a right into a shallow hard-coral garden shel- tered from the current—the perfect place for your safety stop.

A forest of purple soft-coral trees flourishes along the north wall of Nasonisoni Passage.

25 Dreadlocks

In the middle of Savusavu Bay, this site is a haven for macro-life lovers.

The site centers on two round bommies that top out at 5m and touch bottom at 20m. Between the two bommies is a 70m swim over a flourishing, pristine hard-coral garden, home to lionfish, harlequin filefish and butterflyfish. Each bommie is topped with lush hard-coral growth, while the sides are lavishly festooned with soft corals—a band of multicolored soft corals from 7 to 9m and a blanket of yellow soft corals from 9m to the seafloor.

Within this profusion of color, you'll find several species of vividly hued flatworms and nudibranchs, the latter often among the sponges along the bommie sides. Watch for the resident lionfish and spotted sweetlips that shelter in the bommies' numerous overhangs.

Location: Savusavu Bay

Depth Range: 5-20m (15-65ft)

Access: Boat

Expertise Rating: Novice

Macro life includes otherworldly nudibranchs.

Risky Business

European traders flocked to Fiji in the early 19th century to procure the lucrative *bêche-de-mer* (sea cucumber). It fetched huge profits in Asia, where it is considered a delicacy and aphrodisiac.

You are likely to see some of these ugly slug-like creatures while diving or snorkeling. They feed on organic matter in the sand and serve an important role as cleaners in the lagoon ecosystem. There are various types: Some are smooth and sticky, some prickly, some black and some multicolored. After being cut open and cleaned,

they are boiled to remove the salt, then sun-dried or smoked. Many find the taste revolting, but it is highly nutritious, with 50% to 60% protein.

Bêche-de-mer is still a lucrative commodity, both for local use and for export, and unscrupulous traders are delivering dive equipment to residents in remote areas and promising high rewards. Villagers of the Bua region in southwest Vanua Levu are renowned for harvesting the creature. Usually untrained and unaware of the risks, they are encouraged by the traders to dive in deep waters, risking their health and lives by using faulty or dirty air-compression equipment. Many end up with the bends and a stint in the Fiji Recompression Chamber, and several have died.

26 Barracuda Point

This dive starts on a reef wall just offshore from the Cousteau Island Resort.

Location: South of Savusavu Bay

Depth Range: 15-25m (50-80ft)

Access: Boat

Expertise Rating: Intermediate

Keeping the wall to your right, drop down to about 17m, where a hard-coral reef finger extends out 100m, gradually sloping down to 25m. As you swim down this finger, you'll soon join a school of 50 to 60 resident barracuda that like to hover above the reef.

At the tip of the finger, the reef suddenly drops away, and you'll likely notice more of a current running. Sea fans and staghorn coral thrive along the edge of the finger, and you may spot several hammerheads and schools of batfish. There is even a batfish cleaning station near a cluster of staghorn coral, and the batfish allow underwater photographers to come in close for a shot. Finish your dive by returning to the wall, slowly working your way up to 5m for your safety stop.

Swim with squadrons of schooling barracuda for a predator's perspective of the reef.

27 Dreamhouse

This small submarine seamount is considered one of southern Vanua Levu's top dive sites, known for pelagic encounters. Descend from the permanent mooring onto the current-exposed part of the wall, which begins at 10m. From there you can hit your desired depth and watch the big boys go by.

If the current is running, the best thing to do is visit a range of depths in the flow zone. Frequent visitors include a school of 15 to 20 small grey reef sharks, along with a few larger individuals. Sightings of oceanic whitetips are less common, but divers regularly spot tiger sharks and schools of as many as 60 hammerheads. Besides these adrenaline-pumping shark encounters, you may spot other pelagics such as walu, kingfish, jacks and tuna and enjoy an

Location: East of Savusavu Bay

Depth Range: 10-40m+ (35-130ft+)

Access: Boat

Expertise Rating: Intermediate

array of multihued soft corals and broad sea fans.

If the current is not running, the plan is to circumnavigate the seamount. In 30 to 40 minutes you'll complete the circle, while marveling at smaller tropical reef fish, a variety of hard corals and a blue adhesive anemone at the 15m mark. This plate-sized anemone is populated by a pair of popcorn shrimp, making for excellent macrophotography.

Popcorn shrimp shelter among the stinging tentacles of an adhesive anemone.

Namena

This small island is 25km (16 miles) off the southeastern coast of Vanua Levu. Typical of the South Pacific dream image, it boasts lush green hills, palm-fringed golden beaches and some of Fiji's very best diving. Here the most spectacular soft-coral formations are found in very shallow water, swirling with thousands of orange, pink and red fairy basslets, making it an underwater photographer's delight. The water is usually clear, but currents are generally strong. Diving is possible via live-aboards and the resident resort, Moody's Namena.

28 Fantasea

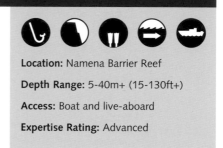

This is a huge area with variable terrain, beginning with a wall that drops from 4m into the deep and then opens up into a wide channel. While the shallows are a bit barren, impressive clusters of pink sea fans embellish the wall and its many cuts below 20m.

Location: Namena Barrier Reef

Depth Range: 5-40m+ (15-130ft+)

Access: Boat and live-aboard

Expertise Rating: Advanced

Once you're over the top of the wall, there's usually no going back, as the currents tend to be strong. You'll be swept into a channel chock-full of bommies covered with soft corals in all shades of color. The countless bommies are abuzz

Constellations of colorful basslets fan out over the barrier reef's countless bommies.

with thousands of brilliant basslets—a simply overwhelming sight. This is a good spot to employ a reef hook, gain neutral buoyancy, hang in the current and let all the action happen around you. Sea snakes, lionfish, sharks and fusiliers are all actively feeding and moving about when a current is running.

Amid the bommies is a vast sand patch, an underwater Sahara that is home to at least two rare sand-diver species.

29 Thumbs Up

Along the southern edge of Namena Barrier Reef, this spot consists of several small, sheer-sided pinnacles known as chimneys.

Each chimney rises from 24m to within a few meters of the surface and is endowed with a truly astonishing array of soft corals, sea fans and crinoids. Numerous undercuts slice deeply into the rock at various depths, sheltering brilliant coral trout, Tahitian squirrelfish and hingebeak shrimp. Take care not to break off any coral branches as you look for little critters, as the undercuts are densely overgrown with orange, red and pink soft corals and sea fans. Several small crevices are home to scarlet cleaner shrimp, which are more than willing to give divers a thorough dental cleaning. Look closely to spot a variety of unusual and very colorful nudibranchs.

In the shallows atop the bommies, you'll find anemones, arceye and flame hawkfish, freckled blennies and swirling basslets. Occasionally, manta rays will cruise over the pinnacles in the shallows.

Location: Namena Barrier Reef

Depth Range: 3-24m (9.8-80ft)

Access: Boat and live-aboard

Expertise Rating: Novice

Another satisfied customer visits the cleaning station.

30 North Save-a-Tack

This huge, world-class dive site encompasses North Save-a-Tack Passage, a wide channel speckled with bommies covered in soft corals. The dive generally starts on the seaward side of the channel, where a wall drops into blue water. You'll descend onto a white-sand seafloor that gently slopes down to the top of the wall at 30m. Here barracuda, jacks and tuna, schooling hammerheads, giant marbled rays, huge groupers and grey reef sharks are among the residents.

Location: North Save-a-Tack Passage

Depth Range: 5-40m+ (15-130ft+)

Access: Boat and live-aboard

Expertise Rating: Advanced

After interacting with the big boys, turn around and swim toward the bommies. The first one you'll likely reach is spanned by a large arch, with an overhang that houses several spotted sweetlips. All of the bommies are blanketed in soft corals of all shades. You may see sea snakes, whitetip reef sharks, more large groupers and lots of colorful butterflyfish and angelfish roaming about. In the vast sand and rubble patches separating the bommies, you'll find lots of large triggerfish, a variety of gobies and garden eels, including a spectacular unnamed species with orange bands.

Tread carefully during the nesting season of both titan and yellowmargin triggerfish (usually November). These two species build their nests among the rubble, and when guarding their eggs, the females of each species become very aggressive. They are known to chase divers and even occasionally bite them! If you are attacked, beat a retreat and avoid the rubble patches.

Continuing through the channel, you may end up at a shallow bommie nicknamed "Kansas" for its prolific coating of a species of leather coral that resembles a field of wheat swaying in the wind. Kansas is frequently current-swept, and the soft-coral growth covering its sides is truly mind-boggling. Amid this profusion of color, you'll spot magnificent anemones, bubble coral, small sea fans and myriad colorful fish. A small bommie beside Kansas features the "Window of Dreams," a large opening clustered with soft corals, sea fans and various types of whip coral.

Huge bottom-dwelling groupers roam the seafloor.

Taveuni Dive Sites

Blessed with lush rainforests, cascading waterfalls and the ever-present fragrance of tropical blossoms, Taveuni is known as the Garden Island. In the center of this elongated island towers a mountain ridge that includes two of Fiji's highest peaks: Des Voeux, at 1,195m, and Mount Uluigalau, at 1,241m. The ridge runs perpendicular to the southeasterly prevailing winds, gathering clouds at the summit and allowing for abundant rainfall, especially on the windward side. Due to its stunning natural beauty, the island is particularly popular with hikers, nature lovers and divers.

Taveuni

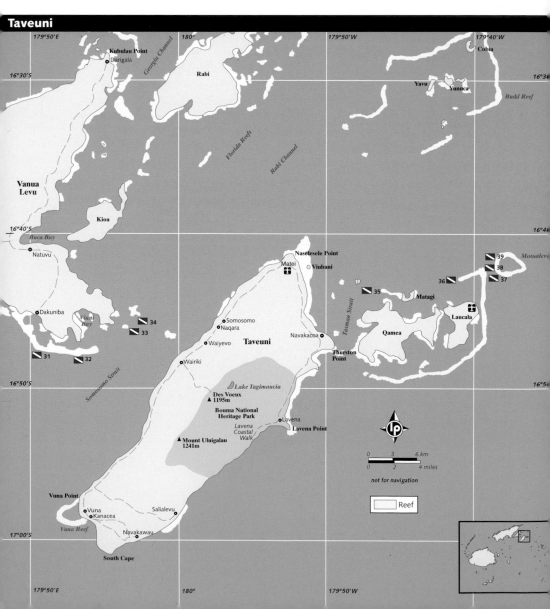

The prime dive sites are between Taveuni and Vanua Levu in the Somosomo Strait, an area that contributed to Fiji's early reputation as the world's soft-coral capital. Visibility in the Somosomo Strait is variable, and divers should prepare for strong currents. There are also world-class dive sites around neighboring Matagi, Qamea and Laucala Islands and at Motualevu atoll, which boasts excellent visibility and mild currents.

Taveuni is blessed with natural beauty both on land and underwater.

Taveuni Dive Sites

	Good Snorkeling	Novice	Intermediate	Advanced
31 Purple Wall				●
32 Great White Wall				●
33 Rainbow Passage				●
34 Annie's Bommies			●	
35 Stillwater			●	
36 Bonnie's Boulder		●		
37 Yellow Wall			●	
38 The Edge			●	
39 Noel's Wall			●	

31 Purple Wall

Purple Wall is on the outskirts of Somosomo Strait, just off the eastern-most point of Vanua Levu. This stunning wall dive derives its name from the uniformly hued coral growth. Dense foliage of soft-coral trees, whip corals and sea fans display all possible shades of purple, making for a very unique dive site.

Location: Somosomo Strait

Depth Range: 11-18m (35-60ft)

Access: Boat and live-aboard

Expertise Rating: Advanced

Currents can be swift, but generally dissipate as you drop below the top of the wall.

Besides the magnificent coral growth, this is a great site to encounter manta rays, barracuda and a wealth of tropical fish. Numerous overhangs and arches throughout the dive site shelter soldier-fish, squirrelfish and multicolored soft coral.

Despite cyclone damage to the shallow hard-coral gardens over the years, there is still plenty of interesting marine life to observe. While doing your safety stop, watch for resident scorpionfish and a variety of wrasses.

Teeming with life, the wall is painted in purple corals and sea fans.

32 Great White Wall

At the entrance to narrow, current-swept Somosomo Strait, Great White Wall has long been one of Fiji's most famous dive sites. In a region of dive site superlatives, Great White Wall remains a unique and awesome wall dive, with its uniformly white soft-coral growth, resembling a steep, snow-covered ski slope. The white coral trees give off an iridescent laven-der sheen, perhaps due to the significant depth the coral thrives in.

Location: Somosomo Strait

Depth Range: 9-40m+ (30-130ft+)

Access: Boat and live-aboard

Expertise Rating: Advanced

This underwater winter wonderland begins at 25m and drops off well beyond the recreational dive limit. This vertical drop-off plummets dramatically into the deep blue and is frequented by swift currents, requiring advanced diving skills. Neutral buoyancy is a must, and you should monitor your gauges closely throughout the dive to avoid straying too deep.

Higher up, at the 15m mark, is the opening to a swim-through cave. Divemasters often begin the dive by leading their groups through this cave, pointing out the resident lionfish and squirrelfish. The tunnel-like swim-through drops down to 25m, spilling you out on the vertical wall atop the snowy slope, where myriad squarespot anthias swirl across the fields of white coral.

Fields of white soft coral appear iridescent lavender at depth.

33 Rainbow Passage

This legendary site features a large, sub-merged reef offering an array of marine life, incredible soft-coral growth and pelagic encounters. It can easily be split up over a number of dives.

Several bommies protrude from the reef, each one spectacularly ornamented

Location: Somosomo Strait

Depth Range: 5-40m+ (15-130ft+)

Access: Boat

Expertise Rating: Advanced

Strong currents support a wealth of marine life.

with soft-coral trees in every color of the rainbow. Thousands of orange and multi-hued fairy basslets swirl among the branches of these trees, setting the whole reef into motion. Look closely to find multitudes of crinoids, Christmas tree worms, flatworms, nudibranchs, clown triggerfish and other tropicals. You'll also spot a number of anemones and sea whips nestled within this forest, and if you have a keen eye, you may even spot the resident stonefish.

Don't forget to think big, as in most areas of Rainbow Reef you can en-counter kingfish, barracuda, whitetip reef sharks and, with a bit of luck, even leopard sharks.

34 Annie's Bommies

In the heart of Somosomo Strait is a submerged reef formed by several big bommies, each dripping with a profu-sion of soft-coral gardens and swirling basslets. When the current is running, literally every inch is suffused with a flower-like beauty spanning the color spectrum. Divers manage the current by weaving in and out of the bommies.

While this is one of the few sites in the region that lacks the drama of a vertical wall, you may appreciate the opportunity to leisurely meander along the bottom.

Location: Somosomo Strait

Depth Range: 5-21m (15-70ft)

Access: Boat and live-aboard

Expertise Rating: Intermediate

Marvel at the luxuriant colors while also scanning the seafloor for leopard sharks, stingrays, moray eels or macro critters such as pipefish and gobies.

At Annie's Bommies, a long-jawed squirrelfish lays low while dozens of basslets ride the current.

35 Stillwater

In spite of its name, this site experiences very strong currents more often than not. In fact, this reef was once home to a beautiful hard-coral garden that was later tumbled and largely destroyed by cyclones. It is once again an outstanding dive, however, as incredible forests of soft coral have since established themselves on the shattered hard-coral base.

Perched along a gently sloping wall, large clusters of white, pink, red, orange, lavender and purple soft corals blend

Location: Qamea Island

Depth Range: 6-24m (20-80ft)

Access: Boat

Expertise Rating: Intermediate

together into a multicolored mélange. Anemones also dot the reef, some wreathed in soft coral, making for world-class photo ops.

As you continue along the wall, you'll drift past numerous large sea fans at the 20m mark and below, eventually reaching a pair of protruding bommies that top out at 5m and drop down to 12m. These bommies are blanketed in purple and red soft corals and abuzz with thousands of orange basslets.

Splendid soft corals thrive atop Stillwater's storm-damaged hard-coral base.

36 Bonnie's Boulder

Bonnie's Boulder is a large shallow pinnacle surrounded by several small coral heads, offering a mix of hard and soft corals and pelagic sightings. Although the coral growth is not as dense and healthy as at other sites, this spot is ideal for novice divers, beginning photographers and anyone else looking for an easy shallow dive in moderate currents.

Where you first enter the water, the soft-coral growth is by far the most lush. Layers of pristine staghorn coral and colorful soft coral cover one small formation, and the main pinnacle is topped by a hard-coral garden, which gives way to coral rubble that slopes into a sandy

Location: Laucala barrier reef

Depth Range: 5-20m (15-65ft)

Access: Boat

Expertise Rating: Novice

bottom at 20m. You'll find soft-coral formations throughout the site, including arches draped in rainbow hues.

Also watch for the big stuff. Whitetip reef sharks often cruise past the coral heads, as well as the occasional sea snake and leopard shark.

37 Yellow Wall

On the west side of Motualevu atoll, this spectacular sheer wall is covered with golden-yellow soft coral from as shallow as 7m all the way down past 30m. Visibility tends to be crystal clear, providing for exceptional diving conditions.

Location: Motualevu

Depth Range: 5-40m+ (15-130ft+)

Access: Boat

Expertise Rating: Intermediate

Along the wall you'll find a number of overhangs, windows and arches, all lavishly decorated with not only the yellow coral, but also scarlet-red bunches of sea whips, encrusting sponges and multicolored crinoids, making for wonderful photo opportunities. While cruising along the wall, you may spot schooling barracuda and jacks and the occasional walu.

Approaching the end of your dive, you'll find that the top of the wall boasts a nice hard-coral garden, interspersed with white-sand patches. This is a great area to find nudibranchs, shrimp gobies, dartfish, large puffers and resting whitetip reef sharks.

This sheer wall's overhangs, windows and arches glow with yellow soft coral.

38 The Edge

A neighbor to Yellow Wall, The Edge is another top dive site at Motualevu featuring clear water and a breathtaking vertical drop-off.

You'll see pretty patches of multicolored soft corals everywhere, intermixed with different types of hard corals and a few leather corals. Photographers particularly love the coral-laden overhangs and

Location: Motualevu

Depth Range: 5-40m+ (15-130ft+)

Access: Boat

Expertise Rating: Intermediate

Juvenile clown triggerfish typically swim solo.

windows, which are frequented by queen angelfish, blue-girdled angelfish or the blue-spotted coral trout. Among the diverse coral gardens you'll also find colorful clown triggerfish and yellow trumpetfish, as well as magnificent anemones, sometimes curled up into tan or red silky balls. You may also spot pairs of rabbitfish and the occasional poison-fang blenny mimic, with its lemon-yellow coloration, a subspecies unique to Fiji.

39 Noel's Wall

Named for Noel Douglas, owner of Matangi Island Resort, Noel's Wall is one of the more spectacular sites in northern Fiji. Highlights include crystal-clear water, a sheer wall that seemingly drops into the abyss and soft-coral forests in a range of pastels, vivid reds, orange, white and deep purple. Mingled among this explosion of color are sea whips, sea fans and several overhangs and windows carved into the wall at a variety of depths.

But Noel's Wall is also well known for frequent pelagic encounters. Schooling bronze whalers, jacks, bigeye tuna and sporadic manta fly-bys are all a possibility. This is also a great spot to see humphead wrasses, schooling parrotfish, large queen angelfish and schooling butterflyfish.

Location: Motualevu

Depth Range: 5-40m+ (15-130ft+)

Access: Boat

Expertise Rating: Intermediate

A pretty hard-coral garden in the shallows atop the wall makes for a convenient and interesting safety stop.

A profusion
of color marks the
soft-coral growth
along Noel's Wall.

Kadavu Group & the Great Astrolabe Reef Dive Sites

The Kadavu Group encompasses two main islands, Kadavu and Ono, and several smaller islands.

As the fourth-largest of the Fijian Islands, Kadavu (pronounced Kan-DA-vu) is exceptionally picturesque, with gently rolling green hills taking their turns with steep mountains, all bordering some of Fiji's most beautiful beaches. Due to its mountainous nature, Kadavu lacks a road system to speak of, so transportation around the long and narrow island is accomplished mostly by boat. Although the island is easily reached via a short (30- to 40-minute) direct flight from either Suva or Nadi, Kadavu is not considered one of the hot tourist spots. It has therefore retained a very traditional Fijian culture. This, along with fabulous diving on the surrounding reefs, is one of Kadavu's special attractions.

Ono, a small island just northeast of Kadavu, is the springboard to diving on the Great Astrolabe Reef, a vast barrier reef that hugs these islands. Local chiefs presently permit scuba diving only on the southern part of the reef, though this may change in the future.

Kadavu Group & the Great Astrolabe Reef Dive Sites	Good Snorkeling	Novice	Intermediate	Advanced
40 Bure's Jewel	●	●		
41 Yellow Wall		●		
42 Evil Trench			●	
43 Blue Tang	●	●		
44 Mellow Reef	●	●		
45 Pacific Voyager				●
46 Split Rock			●	
47 Vouwa		●		
48 Broken Stone			●	
49 Filipe's Reef		●		
50 Japanese Garden			●	
51 Purple Wall			●	

Most dive sites in the Kadavu Group are easy to access, with moderate currents and short boat rides. Besides diving and snorkeling, Kadavu is also well known for excellent kayaking opportunities. Shallow reefs and weather-protected bays make kayaking a spectacular way to explore this beautiful island.

Kayakers will appreciate Kadavu's calm bays and shallow reefs.

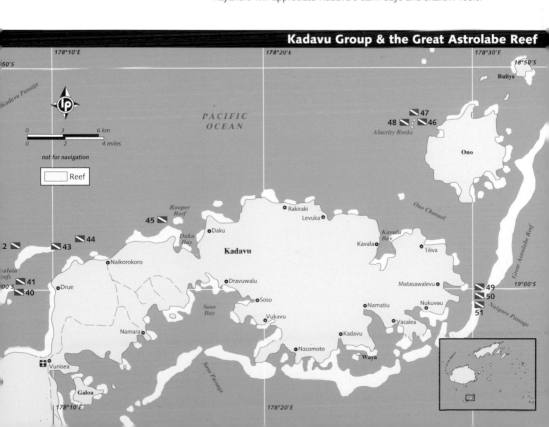

Kadavu Group & the Great Astrolabe Reef

40 Bure's Jewel

Named for a local divemaster, this site comprises a number of shallow, soft-coral endowed bommies that have become very popular with macrophotographers.

Subjects include some of the more flamboyant nudibranchs, commonly found among sea fans and soft corals

Location: Namalata Reefs

Depth Range: 2-25m (6.5-80ft)

Access: Boat

Expertise Rating: Novice

Macro life abounds amid the anemones.

along the sides of the bommies. Several species of anemones bask on the bommies, including carpet and magnificent anemones. Nestled within the velvety tentacles of their stinging hosts, pink and orange-fin anemonefish are both often willing to cooperate for a photograph.

Look closely for other, often-camouflaged macro critters such as scorpionfish, cowrie shells and pipefish. Scrutinize the crinoids, and often you'll find a variety of animals living inside—colorful little lobsters, shrimp that mimic the color of the crinoids and little clingfish all make for intriguing macrophotography. Hard-coral gardens atop the bommies are home to arceye hawkfish, the magnificent flame hawkfish and leopard blennies.

41 Yellow Wall

The heart of this dive site is a narrow cut between two neighboring bommies. Inside the cut, bright yellow stubby soft corals blanket the facing sides of the bommies. You'll also find an array of swim-throughs, windows and undercuts, all beautifully embellished with the signature yellow soft coral, making for a magical dive and plenty of photo opportunities. In fact, this beautiful location has graced the pages and covers of various magazines.

Location: Namalata Reefs

Depth Range: 9-26m (30-85ft)

Access: Boat

Expertise Rating: Novice

Surrounding the vibrant bommies is a coral reef interspersed with rubble patches. This area usually proves to be an excellent place to encounter reef sharks, lionfish and humongous spiny pufferfish.

If you are into macrophotography, you'll likely find several pairs of fire dartfish, sand perches and slingjaw wrasses. You may also spot thicklip wrasses, which stand out due to their intricate facial patterns in an assortment of pastels.

The signature soft coral coats every surface of this cut between neighboring bommies.

42 Evil Trench

This dramatic site is on the outer rim of the barrier reef, with several bommies near the wall edge, just short of the 200-fathom mark. Here you are likely to spot grey and whitetip reef sharks, find yourself engulfed by schools of jacks and barracuda or encounter passing pelagics.

As you continue down the wall, you'll pass several spectacular swim-throughs laced with colorful soft corals and gorgonian sea fans.

At 36m is the entrance to a tunnel that will take you down to 45m, then spill you out on the sheer wall. This is another

Location: Namalata Reefs

Depth Range: 9-40m+ (30-130ft+)

Access: Boat

Expertise Rating: Intermediate

great spot to see sharks and other large fish, but be sure to monitor your depth and air pressure. Only advanced divers should enter the tunnel, due to its significant depth.

43 Blue Tang

Your dive begins atop a coral bommie a meter below the surface. A quick glance and you'll soon realize how the site got its name. The shallows are awash in legions of vibrant blue tangs, which are, oddly enough, only abundant in the vicinity of this one bommie.

Drop down to the rubble bottom on the deeper side, at about 15m, and start looking for the resident ribbon eels. On the shallower side of the bommie, at approximately 12m, you'll find a pretty swim-through laced with sea fans that harbors several large lionfish. This side of the bommie is covered with multihued soft-coral trees, offering great wide-angle photo ops.

Location: Namalata Reefs

Depth Range: 1-18m (3.3-60ft)

Access: Boat

Expertise Rating: Novice

As you cross the rubble field to the neighboring bommies, you are likely to encounter grey reef sharks, schooling trevallies, barracuda and the like. There are several bommies in the vicinity, all boasting lush soft-coral growth. To avoid strong currents, you should only dive this site at the top or bottom of the tide.

44 Mellow Reef

As its name implies, Mellow Reef is an easy site, well suited even to new divers. Although currents can be very strong at times, divers generally only attempt the site at the top or bottom of the tide, to avoid fighting the flow.

The reef consists of several bommies, most approximately 20m across, ranging in depth from 3 to 15m. As you swim from one bommie to the next, you'll cross wide sand and rubble patches that

Location: Namalata Reefs

Depth Range: 3-19m (9.8-60ft)

Access: Boat

Expertise Rating: Novice

host large harems of exquisite wrasses. Usually hovering within a meter of the rubble, the male wrasses are often on display, flashing their magnificent color patterns. To catch the show, look about 5m ahead. Once you spot a school of wrasses, carefully settle on the sandy bottom, wait for the wrasses to get used to you, then inch your way ringside.

The sand patches are also home to the beautiful purple fire goby and a variety of dartfish, including zebra and spot-tail dartfish.

Male exquisite wrasses put on a show.

The Battle of the Shark & Octopus Gods

Dakuwaqa the Shark God once cruised the Fijian islands, challenging other reef guardians. On hearing that a monster in Kadavu waters was reportedly stronger than himself, he sped down to the island to disprove the rumor. Dakuwaqa came across the giant octopus and adopted his usual battle strategy of charging with his mouth wide open and sharp teeth prepared. The octopus, however, anchored itself to the coral reef and swiftly wrapped its free tentacles around the shark's body and jaws, clasping the shark in a death lock. Dakuwaqa was rendered helpless and had to beg for mercy. In return for lenience, the octopus demanded that his subjects, the people of Kadavu, be forever protected from shark attack. In Kadavu, the people now fish without fear and regard the shark as their protector. Most won't eat shark or octopus out of respect for their gods.

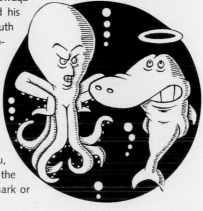

MICK WELDON

45 *Pacific Voyager*

This 63m-long tanker was purposely sunk in 1994 as an artificial reef after being stripped of all doors and equipment that could present a danger to divers. She now rests on her side in 30m of water. Penetration of the vast holds, wheelhouse and crew quarters is possible.

Location: Rooper Reef

Depth Range: 24-30m (80-100ft)

Access: Boat

Expertise Rating: Advanced

Many species of fish are flocking to the wreck, including juveniles and species rarely seen on the open reef due to lack of shelter. A careful observer may spot several types of shrimp, nudibranchs and other invertebrates along the ship's hull. Cleaner shrimp frequently dart around the door and window frames, and you're likely to spot a 1m coral trout that makes its home near the bow anchor well.

With such an abundance of resident critters, this dive is a macrophotographer's heaven. Hard and soft corals already paint the hull, and as with any artificial reef, life will only get better.

A nudibranch's bold colors warn fish of its bitter taste.

46 Split Rock

This site is on the western side of the Great Astrolabe Reef, where it breaks up into a network of passages and small reef structures known as the Alacrity Rocks. It features a maze of submerged pinnacles profusely honeycombed with swim-throughs, caverns, splits and canyons. While the outside of the pinnacles supports minimal coral growth—limited to a stubby soft-coral species that reflects an uncommon bluish color—soft corals and sea fans brilliantly color the inside of the various cavern formations.

One particularly large split between two of the pinnacles, some 6m wide and 15m high, boasts a number of huge red gorgonian fans. Within this split you'll find numerous windows, crevices and

Location: Alacrity Rocks

Depth Range: 6-24m (20-80ft)

Access: Boat

Expertise Rating: Intermediate

overhangs, all blanketed with an unusual encrusting sponge that thrives in pink, purple, white and yellow.

Several colonies of the pretty strawberry anemone perch atop the rocky pinnacles, along with their symbiotic partners, the red-and-black anemonefish. The shallows also draw schooling fusiliers and juvenile purple basslets.

Wend your way through the main split to find arrays of encrusting sponges and red sea whips.

47 Vouwa

Amid the Alacrity Rocks, northwest of Ono Island, Vouwa includes a large number of tightly grouped bommies crisscrossed with steep, twisting canyons. Within these canyons, you will likely encounter some current, along with a profusion of lush coral growth.

Location: Alacrity Rocks

Depth Range: 6-18m (20-60ft)

Access: Boat

Expertise Rating: Novice

There are several beautiful wide-angle setups for underwater photographers, with kaleidoscopic combinations of soft corals, huge sea fans and crinoids. Look for yellow or speckled trumpetfish among the branches of the sea fans. You may also spot large schools of jacks, as well as walu, barracuda and other pelagics. Search the rubble surrounding the bommies for dragon wrasses, yellowtail coris, shrimp gobies and fire dartfish.

Despite the current, this is generally an easy dive that novice and experienced divers alike will enjoy.

Soft corals and crinoids form beautiful bouquets.

48 Broken Stone

Broken Stone is in the same locale as Split Rock and Vouwa. All three sites have similarities, but Broken Stone stands out with a truly awesome cavern formation.

Formed by four bommies nearly equal in size, the site is honeycombed with canyons, tunnels, arches and windows. The centerpiece is a skylighted cavern in the middle of the maze. Along its walls are several undercut shelves alive with sea whips, soldierfish and lobsters, while

Location: Alacrity Rocks

Depth Range: 1-15m (3.3-50ft)

Access: Boat

Expertise Rating: Intermediate

several small cracks and one large skylight pierce the ceiling. At noon, when the sun is high, dancing rays of sunlight flood through these openings and sparkle across the sandy seafloor.

Outside the maze, along the bommie walls, you'll see small schools of vibrant two-spot snappers, tangs and wrasses. Soft coral and sea fans are a bit more sparse than at the other two sites, but there are patches of the same unusual encrusting sponge as at Split Rock.

At the heart of Broken Stone is this mystical, skylighted cavern, a temple to the sun.

49 Filipe's Reef

Named after local divemaster Filipe, this reef is along the inner wall of the Great Astrolabe Reef near Naiqoro Passage. The spot is sheltered from wind and ocean swells and makes for a great dive when the weather will not cooperate. It's also an ideal reef for novice divers and macrophotographers.

Location: Naiqoro Passage

Depth Range: 6-24m (20-80ft)

Access: Boat

Expertise Rating: Novice

Divers usually drop directly down to 12m, where an awesome grass-green lettuce coral patch offers a distinct contrast to the white-sand bottom and rich blue water. Scattered over the gently sloping bottom are stands of stunning antler, staghorn and table coral. You'll likely spot a variety of damselfish, constantly darting in and out of the coral branches. Also prevalent are parrotfish, huge coral trout and other groupers, and you may even spot such delicate beauties as the harlequin ghost pipefish.

As you drift toward the passage, you'll notice scattered coral formations giving way to a wall and thicker stands of hard coral. You'll also encounter large schools of teardrop and Pacific double-saddle butterflyfish.

A massive patch of lettuce coral shelters several tropical species.

50 Japanese Garden

On the north side of Naiqoro Passage, Japanese Garden is a drift dive along a wall.

Although the wall doesn't boast as dense a soft-coral garden as neighboring Purple Wall—instead featuring hard corals and the occasional sea fan—the deeper, seaward side of the channel is

Location: Naiqoro Passage

Depth Range: 5-36m (15-120ft)

Access: Boat

Expertise Rating: Intermediate

blessed with spectacular soft-coral growth. Here huge red, purple and bright-orange trees grow from the rubble seafloor like a fairy-tale forest. At this depth, you'll need a light to truly appreciate the wide range of colors.

Whitetip reef sharks roam the wall, as do large spiny puffers, sea snakes and schooling fusiliers. You'll also encounter a variety of butterflyfish, batfish and the stunning emperor angelfish.

You'll need a light to bring out the vibrant colors of such soft-coral trees.

51 Purple Wall

When the current is running, Purple Wall is definitely one of Kadavu's more adrenaline-pumping dives. The wall forms the south side of Naiqoro Passage, a narrow channel frequently swept by strong tidal currents. Ideally, diving takes place during an incoming current.

Location: Naiqoro Passage

Depth Range: 5-36m (15-120ft)

Access: Boat

Expertise Rating: Intermediate

The wall drops vertically to about 21m, then gradually slopes until it meets the sandy channel floor at 36m. The shallows are festooned with hard corals, anemones and soft corals of various shades, with purple predominating. Between 10 and 20m the channel wall is dotted with large patches of purple soft corals. You'll also find whip coral gardens and plenty of large sea fans, their brilliant reds subdued at depth. In the deeper water, stands of huge soft-coral trees forest the seafloor.

Throughout your dive you'll see large red snappers, sweetlips and juvenile black snappers along the wall, while schools of skittish paddletail snappers cruise the shallows.

A forest of massive soft-coral trees sprouts from the seafloor in Naiqoro Passage.

This deepwater expanse is famous for its seamounts.

The vast region of Bligh Water encompasses the area between Viti Levu and Vanua Levu and reaches almost all the way from the Yasawas to Makogai Channel. This largely unexplored region consists mostly of deep water, with only a sprinkling of islands and few reef structures shallow enough for divers. For the purpose of this book, Bligh Water is largely confined to reefs and seamount formations near Vatu-i-ra Channel.

The now world-famous Bligh Water dive site E6 was discovered by Rob Barrel of Nai'a Cruises when he chartered a plane in 1994 to search for whales. As the massive seamount almost

Bligh Water Dive Sites

	Good Snorkeling	Novice	Intermediate	Advanced
52 Rawai's Wives			●	
53 Nai'a Flaya				●
54 Cat's Meow			●	
55 Rob's Knobs		●		
56 E6		●	●	
57 Mount Mutiny (Hi8)		●		●
58 Vatu-i-cake			●	

breaks the surface at low tide, it was clearly visible from the air. Rob has continued to explore this remote region and has discovered a series of dives that rank among the very best in Fiji, if not worldwide. Other live-aboards have followed, making some of the prime sites accessible to more divers. Even some land-based operators are able to reach a couple of the sites—weather and water conditions permitting.

Because most dive spots in Bligh Water are located far from the main islands and, thus, the effects of river runoff, you can normally expect very clear water.

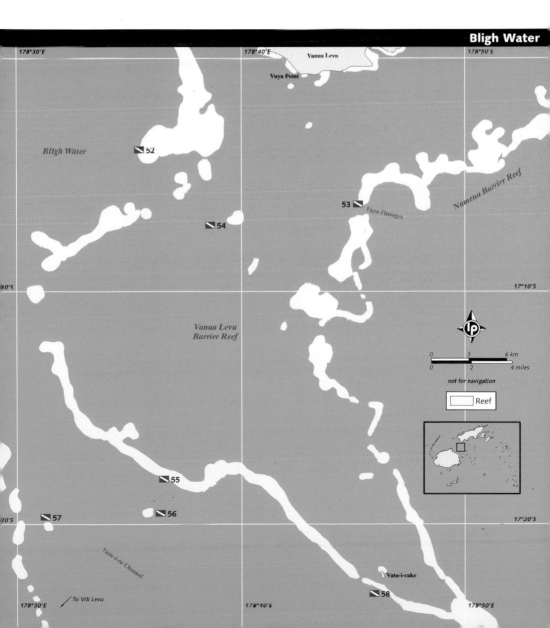

Dealing with Currents

Currents in Fiji are variable, ranging from totally absent to raging 4-knot flows. (A knot is equal to 1.9km/h or 1.2mph.) Methods of dealing with currents include avoiding or escaping from them or simply drifting with them. Since currents are usually associated with tidal movement, they are generally more apparent at the surface than in deeper water. Often you can escape a current by simply dropping below it.

Ebb currents, occurring close to the edge of a wall, often run perpendicular to the length of the wall, pushing you up or down its face. With this type of current, it usually works best if you hug the wall. Move within a foot of the wall, taking advantage of every outcropping you can tuck behind, until you notice the current subsiding, which is often the case after only a few meters.

In general, avoid swimming against a current. Go with the flow whenever possible. At times, you might have to swim up-current—if you want to observe shark action or make your way to a dive site, for example. When doing so, move as close to the bottom or wall as possible. Pulling yourself along by grabbing hold of rocks requires a lot less energy (not to mention air) than kicking—but please, do not grab the coral! Coral is far too fragile to withstand the combined force of both your grip and a strong current.

If you carry a bulky camera, especially with long strobe arms and heavy strobes, battling a current becomes an even greater drag. Fold your arms and streamline your camera apparatus as much as possible. Once you're out of the current or in a protected little niche where you can rest and observe marine life, you can readjust your strobes.

52 Rawai's Wives

Three bommies set the stage for this colorful site, each representing one of *Nai'a* captain Rawai's claimed wives. As the bommies stand about 50m from one another, this site is best split up over several dives.

All three "wives" are beautifully adorned with soft corals, sea whips, fans, anemones and swirling lyretail anthias, especially the bright-orange female of the species.

Location: Vanua Levu Barrier Reef

Depth Range: 5-21m (15-70ft)

Access: Live-aboard

Expertise Rating: Intermediate

Perhaps the most spectacular bommie is wife number two. She boasts a 2m wide, ribbon-shaped crack about her middle that runs all the way through the bommie. One side of this passage is lined with yellow soft corals, making for a spectacular swim-through.

During your dive among these bommies, you are likely to see schooling barracuda, roaming whitetips and some fat dogtooth tuna. This is also a great spot to find coral trout, lionfish and nudibranchs. The rubble floor is a good area to photograph shrimp gobies and accompanying blind shrimp, and you may also find pairs of fire dartfish and blackfin dartfish.

Venomous lionfish are often unafraid of divers.

53 Nal'a Flaya

This 300m run through one of the Vuya Passages presents a thrilling drift dive. Your dive begins on the seaward side of the channel, from where you'll drift with the current into the lagoon. As the strong rip makes it virtually impossible for photographers to handle their cameras, it's wiser to simply leave the camera behind this trip.

Where you first drop in, the seafloor supports a giant sea-whip forest, with rods 1 to 2cm thick and up to 3m high. The channel is close to 40m deep here, so watch your gauges—you'll want plenty of bottom time! Make your way toward the side of the channel, formed by a close batch of bommies carpeted from top to bottom with purple and yellow soft corals. Fly by the first bommie, which is about 100m long, and you'll end up in about 20m of water.

Location: Vanua Levu Barrier Reef

Depth Range: 9-39m (30-130ft)

Access: Live-aboard

Expertise Rating: Advanced

From here, hover over the bommies at between 10 to 15m all the way through the channel.

The marine life in this passage is most spectacular when the current is raging. Thousands of anthias swirl over the dense soft-coral carpet, and grey reef sharks, mantas and lionfish are a common sight. As if nature planned this site for divers, a shallow hard-coral garden offers a convenient safety stop at the end of the channel.

54 Cat's Meow

The heart of this large dive area is a shallow reef. One side offers an array of soft, hard and leather corals and sea fans, as well as chances to spot scorpionfish, nudibranchs and flatworms. The other side features hard corals and a shallow rubble bottom. Highlighting the site are two small bommies to the east and west.

The namesake eastern bommie spans from 5 to 21m and is showered

Location: Vanua Levu Barrier Reef

Depth Range: 5-24m (15-80ft)

Access: Live-aboard

Expertise Rating: Intermediate

in spectacular soft corals, sea fans and anemones from top to bottom, resembling a lush flower garden in full bloom. Toward its base, several overhangs and outcroppings make for dramatic window scenes, with dense blankets of golden coral trees tiling the ceilings, and pinks, reds and purples lavishly painting the walls and floors.

The western bommie is called **Humann Nature**, after marine naturalist Paul Humann, who was involved with the discovery of the site. What Humann Nature may lack in soft-coral coverage compared to Cat's Meow, it makes up for in sheer size and diversity. You'll find patches of striking soft corals, pristine hard-coral gardens and coral-lined canyons, as well as crinoid-embellished sea fans scattered across the sloping seafloor. Also look for turtles, large clamshells, mantis shrimp and schooling butterflyfish.

The namesake bommie is abloom with marine life.

55 Rob's Knobs

On the north side of Vatu-i-ra Channel, Rob's Knobs is a huge site that starts in the shallows, with a sharp drop to about 10m. Along this rocky mini-wall are clusters of sea fans and anemones. Look among the anemones for a huge filter-feeding porcelain crab. A gentle slope leads from 10 to 24m before leveling off. Along this slope you'll find unusually pristine and healthy hard-coral growth. Between 15 and 20m you'll also find large colonies of fluorescent-orange zoanthids, tiny anemone-like animals usually found only in small patches of perhaps 10 to 20 polyps.

Also along the slope are bommies of various sizes that feature undercuts, small windows, crevices and nooks. You'll see mostly hard coral and anemones, but some of the bommies also sport an assortment of soft coral. Throughout your dive you may spot mantis shrimp, nudibranchs, flatworms, a school of curious

Location: Vanua Levu Barrier Reef

Depth Range: 6-24m (20-80ft)

Access: Live-aboard

Expertise Rating: Novice

batfish and a vast array of wrasses, butterflyfish and rabbitfish.

A porcelain crab holes up in an anemone's tentacles.

56 E6

This seamount in Vatu-i-ra Channel rises from 1,000m to the surface. Since there is no safe overnight anchorage, diving normally takes place between dawn and dusk. Named after the endless E6 slide processing it has inspired, the site is large enough to be spread out over several dives. Currents tend to be mild.

Boat moorings mark the most enchanting area. Here a large, skylighted cavern named The Cathedral is networked with numerous overhangs and

Location: Vatu-i-ra Channel

Depth Range: 0-40m+ (0-130ft+)

Access: Boat and live-aboard

Expertise Rating: Intermediate

canyons, all lined in stunning gorgonian fans and soft corals. At noon the sun streams through the cracks in the ceiling and lights up the colorful coral growth—a truly ethereal sight. The cavern floor is home to poison-bristle nudibranchs, pipefish and dragonets that commonly court just before sunset. Crevices throughout the cavern shelter lobsters, crab and shrimp.

As you leave the cavern, you'll emerge among large, beautiful soft corals. You're also likely to spot schooling barracuda, jacks and sharks, including a resident hammerhead.

Complicated by surge at times, the top of the pinnacle boasts a spectacular hard-coral garden. On calm days, this is the ideal spot to observe a crimson flame hawkfish, a photogenic freckled blenny or the tiny, filter-feeding hermit crab that makes its home in the abandoned holes of Christmas tree worms.

A soft-coral tree flowers to full glory in The Cathedral.

57 Mount Mutiny (Hi8)

Also known as Hi8 for its appeal to videographers, Mount Mutiny is a sheer-sided seamount that reaches from 1,000m to just below the surface.

A pristine hard-coral garden peppered with magnificent anemones and patches of the common *Dendronephthya* soft corals dominates the shallows. But the true highlight here is Rainbow Wall, a sheer, partially undercut wall sheltering unusual thin-stalked *Siphonogorgia* coral. This soft-coral species only thrives in dimly lit areas and occurs here in vivid shades of bright yellow, purple, pink and white. The coral growth begins at 15m

Location: Vatu-i-ra Channel

Depth Range: 1-40m+ (3.3-130ft+)

Access: Boat and live-aboard

Expertise Rating: Advanced

and reaches well below the recreational dive limit. Due to the water clarity and sheerness of the wall, you must closely monitor your depth, because there will always seem to be another beautiful soft-coral cluster just a little deeper.

This site is also known for encounters with schooling hammerhead sharks, barracuda and small schools of sweetlips. Also look carefully along the wall to spot the spectacular Lori's anthias and the shy multibarred angelfish.

These unusual, wiry *Siphonogorgia* corals flourish in dimly lit areas.

58 Vatu-i-cake

The untouched barrier reef starting at the small island of Vatu-i-cake (Vatu for short) and stretching some 15km southeast is still in its infancy of exploration.

The inside of the reef harbors numerous shallow bommies that can easily be split up over several dives. Although some stretches of the outer wall appear weather-beaten and consist mostly of fire corals, the fringes boast perfect hard-coral gardens that reach from 5m to below 33m. Between 15 and 20m, large patches of soft corals and crinoid-embellished sea fans add vivid color splashes to the pristine reef. In the mid-

Location: Vatu-i-cake Island

Depth Range: 5-40m (15-130ft)

Access: Boat and live-aboard

Expertise Rating: Intermediate

dle of this soft-coral belt, a window protrudes from the sheer wall. Beautifully decorated with soft corals and whip corals, the window also serves as a cleaning station for spotted sweetlips. You're also likely to spot schooling barracuda, fusiliers, tangs and unicornfish.

Lomaiviti Group Dive Sites

The islands of the Lomaiviti Group stretch out to the east of Viti Levu. The current favorite dive sites are around the picturesque islands of Naigani, Wakaya and Gau (pronounced Ngow), although divers continue to explore the group for new sites.

The sites are extremely diverse—from challenging, current-swept channel dives to easy, current-protected bommie dives well suited to novice divers.

Lomaiviti Group

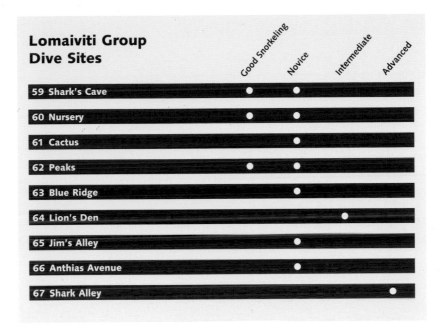

Lomaiviti Group Dive Sites	Good Snorkeling	Novice	Intermediate	Advanced
59 Shark's Cave	●	●		
60 Nursery	●	●		
61 Cactus		●		
62 Peaks	●	●		
63 Blue Ridge		●		
64 Lion's Den			●	
65 Jim's Alley		●		
66 Anthias Avenue		●		
67 Shark Alley				●

Naigani

About 10km (6 miles) off the northeast coast of Viti Levu, near Ovalau, Naigani is a small, picturesque island that sports one resort and dive operation. The diving tends to be very easy, with little current, but visibility can be a bit cloudy due to river runoff whenever eastern Viti Levu receives a lot of rainfall.

59 Shark's Cave

The diving at Shark's Cave revolves around a bommie densely covered with all types of leather corals as well as some soft corals. Atop the bommie is a healthy hard-coral garden that includes several large brain coral formations. Longnose filefish, butterflyfish and schools of fusiliers and jacks are a common sight here.

Location: North of Naigani Island

Depth Range: 5-21m (17-70ft)

Access: Boat

Expertise Rating: Novice

Halfway around this bommie, you'll spot additional bommies in the distance. Swim about 45m in that direction and, after passing several small, fairly barren bommies, you'll arrive at a large bommie with a small split in its side. A whitetip reef shark makes this its home, hence the name Shark's Cave. This second large bommie is not as lush as the first, so after a quick peek to see if the shark is home, you may want to make your way back to the first.

This tends to be an easy dive with little current and is popular with novice divers, including those participating in a resort course.

Look closely amid the hard corals for the longnose filefish.

60 Nursery

Nursery features a bommie encased in lush coral growth. Since the bommie is fairly little, only small groups of divers should descend at a time. Due to the shallow depth and absence of strong currents, novice divers and even resort course divers exploring the underwater world for the first time can enjoy this dive.

Location: North of Naigani Island

Depth Range: 3-21m (9.8-70ft)

Access: Boat

Expertise Rating: Novice

Large brain coral formations, leather corals and huge fields of anemones populate pristine coral gardens in the shallows atop the bommie, while the sides are covered in leather corals. Among the tentacles of the leather corals, look for the dainty floral wrasse and small radial leatherjacket. At about 12m you'll find a large patch of unusual neon-yellow soft coral adorning the ceiling and sides of a window. Look for basslets, colorful wrasses and butterflyfish throughout the dive.

Anemonefish fly in formation across swaying anemone fields atop the bommie at Nursery.

61 Cactus

At Cactus, a narrow channel splits two perfectly round bommies. Both channel sides are elaborately festooned with an exquisite black coral species that has a distinct orange hue. Schools of yellow damselfish and two-spot snappers roam within and around the black coral forest, and some of the trees shelter the magnificent longnose hawkfish. Swirling fusiliers will accompany you throughout the dive.

Location: Offshore from Naigani village

Depth Range: 6-21m (20-70ft)

Access: Boat

Expertise Rating: Novice

At the bottom of the larger bommie, at 21m, a tunnel leads all the way through the formation. The tunnel is wide enough to allow divers to pass through comfortably, and although a light will help you spot critters inside the tunnel, enough natural light is present to easily find the tunnel openings. Large sea fans and colorful soft corals wreathe the tunnel openings and walls. The outside walls of the bommies are decorated with a variety of black coral species starting at 10m and below, while soft-coral trees, leather coral and carpet anemones dominate the shallows.

At Cactus, colorful soft corals coat the tunnel openings and walls.

62 Peaks

Scattered across a rubble bottom are 10 bommies of various sizes, most carved with cracks, crevices and overhangs that are worth checking for critters such as cowries, cleaner shrimp and squirrelfish. You're likely to encounter schools of barracuda, skipjacks, fusiliers and even the occasional walu. This spot also makes an excellent macro dive, as numerous lionfish frequent the bommie walls, along with poison-bristle nudibranchs, shrimp, hermit crab and a variety of shells.

Location: Offshore from Naigani Island Resort

Depth Range: 1-18m (3.3-60ft)

Access: Boat

Expertise Rating: Novice

Although the bommies at Peaks are not as soft-coral intensive as at other

Naigani sites, you will find nice growth throughout your dive. Snorkelers will especially enjoy the hard-coral gardens, consisting of healthy elkhorn and antler corals that grow as shallow as 1 to 5m on some of the bommies.

This is a relatively large site where divers can easily spread out, making it suitable for larger groups. Due to the site's proximity to the resort and the prolific nocturnal marine life, Peaks is also a popular night-diving spot.

Wakaya

Palm trees and a picture-perfect white-sand beach rim Wakaya's lush green hills. A private island, Wakaya hosts an exclusive resort and millionaires' retreat.

Diving is available with the resort's dive boats or via several live-aboards. The visibility is variable and changes with the tides. Currents are generally quite manageable.

63 Blue Ridge

Along the northern edge of Wakaya's sheer outer reef wall, Blue Ridge gains its popularity chiefly from the abundance of bright blue ribbon eels. At least a half dozen of these striking eels make their home between 20 and 24m. Some shelter among the overhangs, so you may need to do a little investigating to find them. Although ribbon eels are known to be shy, a few of them seem to enjoy modeling for photographers, and one has even allowed divers with macro frame setups to snap a picture.

Though the wall sports reasonable coral growth, soft corals are not the main attraction at this site. Instead, divers channel their attention toward the wide variety of fish life. A hammerhead shark has harbored here for many years, along with several manta rays. You may also spot the rare Helfrich's dartfish, the decorated goby and, on

Location: Wakaya wall

Depth Range: 12-40m (40-130ft)

Access: Boat and live-aboard

Expertise Rating: Novice

occasion, even the rufus, or "Irish setter," ghost pipefish.

Adult male ribbon eels are bright blue and yellow.

64 Lion's Den

This site begins where divers normally surface after exploring Blue Ridge. Swim south along the wall until you reach a large cut with a black-sand seafloor. Lionfish are common here and elsewhere along Wakaya wall, and you'll also find several fire and elegant dartfish. With some luck, you may even spot a juvenile ribbon eel. (Juvenile ribbon eels are black with a narrow yellow line, making them less photogenic and much harder to spot than their colorful adult counterparts.)

Location: Wakaya wall

Depth Range: 5-40m+ (15-130ft+)

Access: Boat and live-aboard

Expertise Rating: Intermediate

If you continue to where the wall meets the channel, you'll reach an outcropping known as Yellow Wall, which boasts beautiful yellow soft corals. Don't linger, however, as this small area is quite deep and usually experiences strong currents.

From here, follow the channel into the shallower area. Among the boulder-like bommies you may spot more lionfish, octopuses or one of the resident white-tip sharks. The sand and rubble channel floor is very popular with macrophotographers. If you have a keen eye, you'll find mantis shrimp, many species of shrimp gobies and rare species of nudibranchs. You'll also discover an abundance of leopard sea cucumbers, many living in symbiosis with emperor shrimp and tiny spotted crabs.

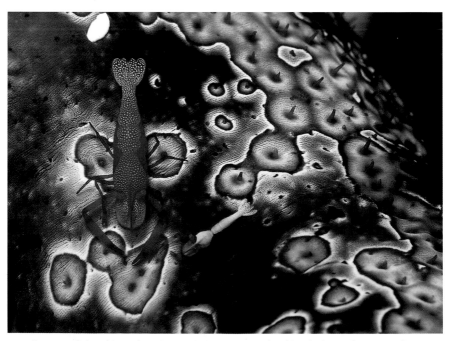

Emperor shrimp forage for microscopic organisms on the skin of a leopard sea cucumber.

Gau

About 50km (30 miles) off Viti Levu's easternmost tip, Gau is Fiji's fifth largest island, yet its lush rolling hills remain largely undeveloped. Diving is generally accomplished from liveaboards. The villagers on Gau always look forward to mixing a good batch of kava and throwing a *meke* (Fijian dance enacting stories and legends) when live-aboard guests stop by for a visit. The diving here is quite diverse—from excellent macro sites with lots of unusual critters to shark-filled channels and pretty coral gardens.

Village visits are a highlight of a trip to Gau.

65 Jim's Alley

Named for well-known photographer Jim Church, Jim's Alley is on the northwest side of Gau's barrier reef.

The site features a series of four bommies that bottom out at 24m, the shallowest reaching to within 5m of the surface. The bommies' numerous undercuts are beautifully lined with black coral trees, soft corals and patches of red whip coral. It's not uncommon to see manta rays here, but this site also boasts a variety of small creatures.

At the edge of the deepest bommie, two striking ribbon eels are among the more popular residents. As you work your way toward the increasingly shallow bommies, you may spot colorful nudibranchs, rare dottybacks, unusual

Location: Gau barrier reef

Depth Range: 5-24m (15-80ft)

Access: Live-aboard

Expertise Rating: Novice

fluorescent anemones, sea snakes and lots of gobies. Keep an eye out for the brilliant longnose hawkfish in the branches of black coral trees. The rubble surrounding the bommies is a good area to look for dragon, moon and checkered wrasses, along with camouflaged bottom dwellers such as lizardfish and sand perches.

66 Anthias Avenue

Two bommies and a large reef structure comprise this popular macro site. Along the sides of the bommies, you'll find a variety of whip corals and a profusion of soft corals populated with pirouetting anthias. On the end of the reef structure at 15m, you can marvel at four ribbon eels that call this site their home. Toward the bottom of the formations, look for a variety of dartfish, unusual nudibranchs, and adhesive anemones hosting photo-

Location: Gau barrier reef

Depth Range: 8-24m (25-80ft)

Access: Live-aboard

Expertise Rating: Novice

Ghost pipefish blend well into their surroundings.

genic popcorn shrimp. Ghost pipefish and the rare rufus ghost pipefish have also been spotted here on occasion.

The tops of the bommies are an equally beautiful and interesting part of this site. Dozens of red-and-black anemonefish tuck into large colonies of bubble-tip anemones that sprout amid hard-coral gardens. Within the tentacles of cauliflower and antler coral, you can find the blood-red flame hawkfish and the eye-catching, yellow and turquoise-checkered longnose filefish. This is also a spot where legions of divers have had their teeth cleaned by the celebrated scarlet cleaner shrimp.

67 Shark Alley

The narrow channel that cuts through Gau's barrier reef is where all the action is. Known as Shark Alley, this passage is frequented by about 20 grey reef sharks, along with marbled groupers and schools of jacks and barracuda.

Both sides of the channel are lined with purple and red soft-coral trees—though when the current is strong, it may be difficult to slow down and appreciate the scenery. You're better off drifting with the current until you reach a Y-junction, where, at about 20m, you can duck

Location: Nigali Passage

Depth Range: 5-27m (15ft-90ft)

Access: Live-aboard

Expertise Rating: Advanced

behind some boulders and watch all the big stuff swim by.

When it's time to ascend to the shallows, hang a right at the Y-junction and drift right over a pristine hard-coral garden. This garden surrounds a huge lettuce coral patch, and if you can manage to battle the current a bit, you'll catch sight of hundreds of sergeants residing among its "leaves." Look carefully into the branching corals surrounding the lettuce patch to spot the lemon-colored fourbar goby, an unusual species that inhabits healthy hard-coral gardens.

Scissor-tail sergeants dodge the current among the leaves of a lettuce coral.

Lau Group Dive Sites

Comprising more than 60 tiny islands scattered across the Koro Sea southeast of Vanua Levu and Viti Levu, the Lau Group officially belongs to Fiji but has nurtured a strong Tongan (Polynesian) influence in the past. Even today, a majority of the islanders speak Tongan as well as Fijian and English. Architecturally, visitors will notice that *bures* (thatched dwellings) are erected in the traditional Tongan style, and some of the people clearly bear Tongan features such as straight hair and lighter skin tones.

The islands themselves are stunning jewels, with powdery white beaches fringed in coconut palms, epitomizing the romanticized image of a South Pacific paradise.

For divers, this remote group with largely unexplored reefs represents one of the last frontiers. For the most part, access is limited to special live-aboard charters. In the north, the *Princess II* visits Wailagi Lala regularly and Vanua Balavu on occasion. On Vanua Balavu, the small Lomaloma Resort also offers diving to certified divers upon prior request. *Nai'a* occasionally offers charters to the Southern Lau Group.

Due to a lack of river runoff from the main islands, the underwater visibility in the Lau Group tends to be excellent and is only occasionally affected by plankton blooms. The reefs host some of the most pristine hard-coral gardens in the world. Soft corals and sea whips occur in some of the deeper sites but are less common than elsewhere in Fiji. Lau also offers encounters with pelagics such as sharks, tuna and even sailfish, though such sightings are far from guaranteed. Success generally requires an experienced guide who is familiar with local currents and their effects on pelagic marine life.

On a remote Lau island beach, yours are the only footprints.

Wailagi Lala

Wailagi Lala is a picture-perfect uninhabited island (*lala* means uninhabited) in the northern Lau Group. It is surrounded by a near-circular reef structure.

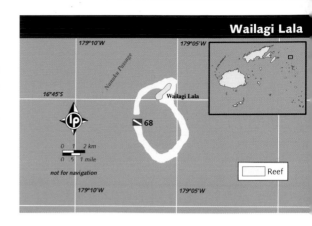

Wailagi Lala Dive Site

	Good Snorkeling	Novice	Intermediate	Advanced
68 Wailagi Lala Passage				●

68 Wailagi Lala Passage

On the west side of the reef, about a quarter mile from Wailagi Lala Island, this passage is the only reef opening, hence the tidal currents can be quite strong. Due to these currents and the significant depth, advanced diving skills are required. Divers normally enter the water on the south side inside the reef and follow the current through the passage to the seaward side.

As you follow the south side of the passage, keep the channel wall to your left. This wall is lined with a spectacular carpet of multihued soft corals, the color purple predominating. When the current is running, you are likely to be greeted by schools of large predators such as barracuda, dogtooth tuna and bronze whalers as you approach the outer reef.

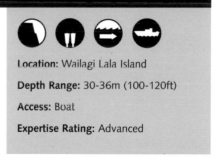

Location: Wailagi Lala Island

Depth Range: 30-36m (100-120ft)

Access: Boat

Expertise Rating: Advanced

Another way to dive the site is to cross the shallow channel about halfway through, finishing your dive on the north wall. The channel floor supports a pristine hard-coral garden with a particularly large and healthy patch of lettuce (or cabbage) coral. Within this patch you may see groupers and sweetlips, while golden trevallies, emperor angelfish, clown triggerfish and butterflyfish also commonly school in the passage. Look carefully at the sand patches amid the hard corals to spot a variety of shrimp gobies and triplefins.

The northern channel wall boasts soft corals, large gorgonian fans and patches of scarlet sea whips. You're also likely to see lionfish, nudibranchs, coral trout, schooling fusiliers and perhaps eagle rays, while reef sharks often roam the waters outside the passage.

Shocks of sea whips sprout from the northern wall.

Vanua Balavu

Vanua Balavu and the eight other small islands within the same large barrier reef system are stunning islands with beautiful white-sand beaches and dramatic limestone cliffs, all surrounded by a turquoise lagoon. The northern tip of this island group is home to the spectacular Bay of Islands, which shelters tiny, mushroom-shaped limestone islands that are every bit as beautiful as the similar world-famous formations in Palau.

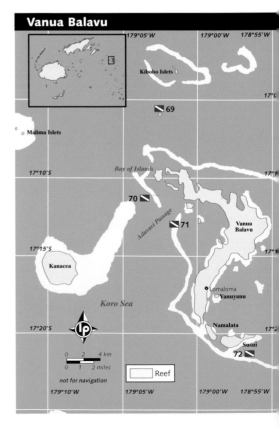

Offshore islands are reminiscent of Palau.

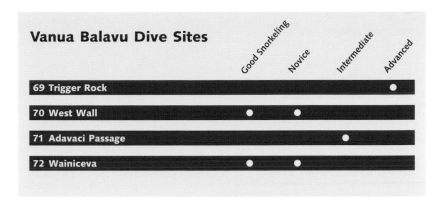

Vanua Balavu Dive Sites

	Good Snorkeling	Novice	Intermediate	Advanced
69 Trigger Rock				●
70 West Wall		●	●	
71 Adavaci Passage			●	
72 Wainiceva		●	●	

69 Trigger Rock

This remote seamount is about 8km north of the northernmost tip of Vanua Balavu—too far to reach by boat from Lomaloma Resort, hence diving is generally done only from live-aboards. For best visibility and a chance at pelagic encounters, this site is best dived on a rising tide.

Location: North of Vanua Balavu Island

Depth Range: 12-27m (40-90ft)

Access: Live-aboard

Expertise Rating: Advanced

Trigger Rock reaches from well below the recreational dive limit to the surface at low tide, but the best range for divers is between 12 and 27m on the sheer northern wall. Here you'll find dense hard-coral growth with colorful splashes of soft coral. Look beneath overhangs wreathed in soft and whip corals to find longjaw squirrelfish, sweetlips, lobsters and the secretive blackspot pygmy wrasses. You'll also find carpet and magnificent anemones with their symbiotic partners—the porcelain crab, tiny shrimp and anemonefish—along with a number of clams, moray eels and the occasional ribbon eel. When the current is running, pelagic fly-bys may include whitetip reef sharks, barracuda and trevallies.

Blackspot pygmy wrasses typically hide in caves and crevices.

70 West Wall

This sheer drop-off is along the outside of Vanua Balavu's western barrier reef and should only be visited when the ocean is relatively calm. Composed of pristine hard corals, the wall reaches from 20m to the surface, making this a prime snorkeling spot as well.

Location: West of Vanua Balavu Island

Depth Range: 0-33m (0-110ft)

Access: Boat

Expertise Rating: Novice

The hard corals differ from those found at neighboring Adavaci Passage and Wainiceva, as the outer wall here is more exposed to swells. Rather than supporting fragile corals such as table coral and species with long branches,

We Prefer Ours Al Dente

One week after the full moon in November, the people of Vanua Balavu witness the annual rising of the *balolo* (tiny green and brown sea worms). At sunrise the Susui villagers collect worms by the thousands. The catch is first soaked in fresh water, then packed into baskets and cooked overnight in a *lovo* (ground oven). The fishy-tasting baked worms are considered a delicacy.

West Wall is home to more robust species such as the hardy cauliflower coral, lobe coral and others sporting thick, short branches.

Multiple gorges and canyons with many overhangs and crevices elaborately cut the shallows. This is a good area to look for lobsters as well as parrotfish and a variety of juvenile wrasses. You'll find most marine life between 6 and 20m. Schooling goatfish and parrotfish, rabbitfish and longfin bannerfish thrive among the coral. You'll also find a number of anemones and the occasional cruising reef shark. A small shelf at 20m offers divers, particularly new divers, a good reference point to check their depth.

71 Adavaci Passage

This dive starts at the channel marker beacon on the south side of Adavaci Passage. You'll descend onto a virgin hard-coral reef comprising massive antler, table and staghorn coral formations. All of them are so fragile yet so perfectly intact, you'll feel like you're swimming through a museum of precious porcelain statues. Both sides of the channel also cultivate an uncommon, aquamarine-blue soft coral found primarily in areas dominated by hard corals.

Location: West of Vanua Balavu Island

Depth Range: 3-30m (9.8-100ft)

Access: Boat

Expertise Rating: Intermediate

Although the wall slopes down to about 30m, there is not much to see below 18m. Most of the coral heads thrive between 3 and 10m, where you're likely to spot numerous whitetip reef sharks along with the typical mix of tropicals. With an incoming current, you may encounter grey reef sharks, walu, tuna and other pelagics in the channel.

Massive stands of fragile staghorn corals thrive on both sides of Adavaci Passage.

72 Waniceva

Between the lee of Susui Island and Vanua Balavu's barrier reef, this hard-coral reef wall drops from the shallows to a white-sand seafloor at 10m. The shallow depth and absence of currents make this site ideal for novice divers and snorkelers.

Divers can explore small coral formations scattered in all directions. You'll find unspoiled hard corals in a wide variety of colors and species. Particularly impressive are the huge, solitary table corals, bluish antler corals and profuse, fragile staghorn corals that thrive in this clear and protected bay. Though not as common as in other areas, anemones

Location: South of Vanua Balavu Island

Depth Range: 0-10m (0-33ft)

Access: Boat

Expertise Rating: Novice

and their symbiotic partners, the anemonefish, are found here in very shallow water and can also be enjoyed by snorkelers. Damselfish and butterflyfish are common visitors to the coral gardens, while lizardfish and gobies scoot along the sandy seafloor.

Fulaga

The crescent-shaped island of Fulaga cradles a lagoon dotted with mushroom-shaped lime-stone islands that rival Palau's in natural beauty. There is only one channel through which boats enter, so be careful when navi-gating the shallow, current-swept passage. Access is by private yacht or specially chartered live-aboards. Be sure to obtain permission from the village chief before doing any diving.

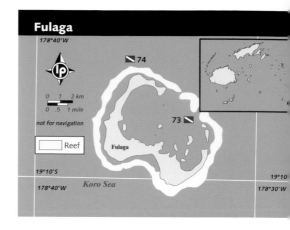

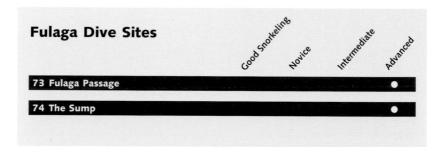

Fulaga Dive Sites

	Good Snorkeling	Novice	Intermediate	Advanced
73 Fulaga Passage				●
74 The Sump				●

Fulaga's lagoon is peppered with fascinating, undercut limestone islands.

73 Fulaga Passage

Best dived during an incoming tide, Fulaga Passage offers a fast and fun ride, with beautiful coral scenery literally flying by below you. Fields of leather coral alternate with purple and green staghorn coral and the odd patch of lettuce coral.

Location: Fulaga Island

Depth Range: 5-40m+ (15-130ft+)

Access: Live-aboard

Expertise Rating: Advanced

On an outgoing tide, once you exit the channel, you can continue your dive south on the outer reef wall. At 25m and below, the wall is decorated with several patches of orange, stubby soft coral. Look for the uncommon Lori's anthias among the trees. Between 10 and 20m, keep your eyes peeled for rainbow runners, schooling barracuda and the occasional wahoo patrolling the wall.

As you work your way up to the shallows, you'll reach a pristine hard-coral garden with numerous inlets that allow you to explore the top of the wall. Here you'll find dragon wrasses, multicolored parrotfish and juvenile butterflyfish, wrasses and damselfish thriving within the protection of the reef.

Dragon wrasses move rocks to find food.

74 The Sump

On the northwest side of Fulaga Island, a gigantic chimney formation is the main draw. Wide enough for several divers to enter at once, the vertical tunnel begins at 20m. Though the tunnel bottoms out at 85m, a hole at 40m allows you to exit without exceeding the recreational diving limit. You'll spill out on the vertical wall amid mind-boggling visibility, often exceeding 50m. Be sure to watch your gauges and begin your ascent as you exit the chimney, as actual depth can be deceiving.

Location: Fulaga Island

Depth Range: 20-40m (66-130ft)

Access: Live-aboard

Expertise Rating: Advanced

Silvertip sharks, wahoos, rainbow runners and other pelagics frequent the wall near the tunnel exit, and as long as you are 25m or deeper, look for Lori's anthias. Flashing emerald-green eyes and striking patterns of orange and purple, these fish frequent slightly undercut areas of steep drop-offs. As you continue your ascent, you'll encounter hard-coral gardens and an endless array of colorful tropicals.

Marine Life

Although Fiji's most famous marine life is its soft coral, the reefs also boast more than a thousand species of fish —some endemic to Fiji—and a great variety of invertebrates. This section identifies some of the species divers are likely to see in Fijian waters, as well as a few rare or simply elusive critters.

If you don't find the species you're looking for on the following pages, ask your dive operator. Most dive resorts and all live-aboards have extensive libraries of fish and invertebrate ID books available for your use.

Keep in mind that common names are used freely by most divers and are often inconsistent. The two-part scientific name is much more accurate. This system is known as binomial nomenclature—the method of using two words (shown in italics) to identify an organism. The first italic word is the *genus*, into which members of similar species are grouped. The second word, the *species*, is the finest detail name and refers to organisms that are sexually compatible and can produce fertile offspring. Where the species is unknown or not yet named, the genus name is followed by *sp.*

Common Vertebrates

red-and-black anemonefish
Amphiprion melanopus

regal angelfish
Pygoplites diacanthus

Lori's anthias
Pseudanthias lori

squarespot anthias
Pseudanthias pleurotaenia

longfin bannerfish
Heniochus acuminatus

bigeye
Priacanthus sp.

poison-fang blenny mimic
Plagiotremus flavus

Pacific double-saddle butterflyfish
Chaetodon ulietensis

leopard coral trout
Plectropomus leopardus

ribbon eel
Rhinomuraena quaesita

longnose filefish
Oxymonacanthus longirostris

harlequin ghost pipefish
Solenostomus paradoxus

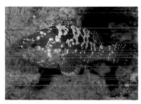

marbled grouper
Epinephelus polyphekadion

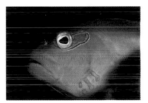

arceye hawkfish
Paracirrhites arcatus

longnose hawkfish
Oxycirrhites typus

red lionfish
Pterois volitans

Schlegel's parrotfish
Scarus schlegeli

spotted porcupinefish
Diodon hystrix

Uspi rabbitfish
Siganus uspi

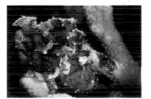

leaf scorpionfish
Taenianotus triacanthus

spotted shrimpgoby
Amblyeleotris guttata

midnight snapper
Macolor macularis

two-spot snapper
Lutjanus biguttatus

blue-spotted stingray
Dasyatis kuhlii

spotted sweetlips
Plectorhinchus picus

clown triggerfish
Balistoides conspicillum

checkerboard wrasse
Halichoeres hortulanus

Common Invertebrates

porcelain crab
Neopetrolisthes oshimai

broadclub cuttlefish
Sepia latimanus

flatworm
Pseudoceros ferrugineus

painted spiny lobster
Panulirus versicolor

nudibranch
Phyllidia pustulosa

octocoral
Sarcophyton sp.

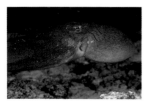
common reef octopus
Octopus cyanea

sea star
Nardoa sp.

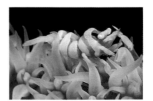
wire coral shrimp
Pontonides unciger

Hazardous Marine Life

Marine animals almost never attack divers, but many have defensive and offensive weaponry that can be triggered if they feel threatened or annoyed. The ability to recognize hazardous creatures is a valuable asset in avoiding injury. Following are some of the potentially hazardous creatures most commonly found in Fiji.

Cone Shells

Do not touch or pick up cone shells. These mollusks deliver a venomous sting by shooting a tiny poison dart from their funnel-like proboscis. Stings will cause numbness and can be followed by muscular paralysis or even respiratory paralysis and heart failure. Immobilize the victim, apply a pressure bandage, be prepared to use CPR, and seek urgent medical aid.

Stonefish

Stonefish, as well as scorpionfish and lionfish, inject venom through dorsal spines that can penetrate booties, wetsuits and gloves. To avoid injury, simply steer clear of these docile creatures. Wounds typically cause intense throbbing pain. Soak the wound in non-scalding hot vinegar or water until the pain subsides. Administer pain medication if necessary. Allergic victims who experience more serious problems such as convulsions or cardiorespiratory failure should be transported to a hospital immediately.

Moray Eel

Distinguished by their long, thick, snake-like bodies and tapered heads, moray eels come in a variety of colors and patterns. Don't feed them or put your hand in a dark hole—eels have the unfortunate combination of sharp teeth and poor eyesight and will bite if they feel threatened. If you are bitten, don't try to pull your hand away suddenly—the teeth slant backward and are extraordinarily sharp. Let the eel release your hand and then surface slowly. Treat with antiseptics, anti-tetanus and antibiotics.

Sea Urchin

There are a variety of sea urchins in Fiji. The type divers should especially avoid is the venomous spiny urchin. These are generally black and white or all black and have very long, brittle spines. The spines are the urchin's most dangerous weapon, easily able to penetrate neoprene wetsuits, booties and gloves. Puncture wounds immediately cause throbbing pain. Since the spines may break off in the flesh, the wound should be monitored for infection. Treat minor punctures by soaking the wound in non-scalding hot water until the pain subsides. More serious injuries require medical attention.

Crown-of-Thorns

This large sea star may have up to 23 arms, although 13 to 18 are more commonly observed. Body coloration can be blue, green or grayish with the spines tinted red or orange. The spines are venomous and can deliver a painful sting even if the animal has been dead for two or three days. Also beware the toxic pedicellariae (pincers) between the spines, which can also cause severe pain upon contact. To treat stings, remove any loose spines, soak stung area in non-scalding hot vinegar or water for 30 to 90 minutes and seek medical aid. Neglected wounds may produce serious injury. If you've been stung before, your reaction to another sting may be worse than the first.

Jellyfish

Jellyfish sting by releasing nematocysts, stinging cells contained in their trailing tentacles. Stings are often just irritating, not painful, but should be treated immediately with vinegar. As a rule, the longer the jellyfish tentacles, the more painful the sting.

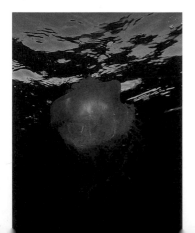

A far greater threat is the Portuguese man-o-war, a distant cousin of the jellyfish that tends to float at the surface and has very long trailing tentacles. Sting symptoms range from a mild itch to intense pain, blistering, skin discoloration, shock, breathing difficulties and even unconsciousness. Remove the tentacles, preferably with tweezers, though anything but bare hands will do. Apply a decontaminant such as vinegar or diluted ammonia and seek immediate medical aid. Allergic reactions can be severe and life-threatening. Luckily, these creatures are only occasionally encountered.

Fire Coral

Although often mistaken for stony coral, fire coral is a hydroid colony that secretes a hard, calcareous skeleton. Fire coral grows in many different shapes, often encrusting or taking the form of a variety of reef structures. It is usually identifiable by its tan, mustard or brown color and finger-like columns with whitish tips. The entire colony is covered by tiny pores and fine, hair-like projections nearly invisible to the unaided eye. Fire coral "stings" by discharging small, specialized cells called nematocysts. Contact causes a burning sensation that lasts for several minutes and may produce red welts on the skin. Do not rub the area, as you will only spread the stinging particles. Cortisone cream can reduce the inflammation, and antihistamine cream is good for killing the pain. A doctor should treat serious stings.

Sea Snake

Air-breathing reptiles with venom that's 20 times stronger than any land snake, sea snakes release venom only when feeding or under extreme distress—so most defensive bites do not contain venom. Sea snakes rarely bite even if they are handled, but avoid touching them. To treat a sea snake bite, use a pressure bandage and immobilize the victim. Try to identify the snake, be prepared to administer CPR, and seek urgent medical aid.

Shark

Tropical shark attacks are very rare—nevertheless, they do occur. Sharks will generally not attack unless provoked, so don't taunt, tease or feed them. Avoid

spearfishing, carrying fish baits or mimicking a wounded fish and your likelihood of being attacked will greatly diminish. Face and quietly watch any shark that is acting aggressively and be prepared to push it away with your camera, knife or tank. If a shark does bite a fellow diver, stop the bleeding, reassure the patient, treat for shock and send for immediate medical help.

Diving Conservation & Awareness

There are no legally recognized marine reserves in Fijian waters, although dive professionals have been trying for years to establish them under the auspices of the Fiji Dive Operators Association. The struggle revolves around traditional fishing rights. Operators must first convince chiefs and villagers not to fish a particular area, and then convince them that divers do not fish or take anything else from the reefs. Of course, divers must honor the pledge to "take only pictures." It has also been difficult for operators to place permanent moorings in some areas, as villagers believe moorings may adversely affect their fishing grounds.

Besides the impact divers and anchors may have, Fiji's hard- and soft-coral reefs are vulnerable to cyclones, crown-of-thorns invasions and coral bleaching. Damage does occur, but currents constantly flush the reefs in nutrient-rich water, speeding their recovery.

Marine Reserves & Regulations

Traditional Fijian fishing rights hinder efforts to secure legal protection for bodies of water. Any activity that might impact a region's fishing grounds must first be approved by a series of clans and their chiefs. Residents of some villages have agreed to no-fishing zones, and neighboring resorts on Beachcomber Island in the Mamanuca Group have protected the reef surrounding that island. But these spots are merely protected areas and not reserves, as they are not safeguarded at the national level.

The most significant protected areas are off Ono Island (near Kadavu) and the Waitabu project on Taveuni. In each instance, fishing and reef walking was banned under traditional village authority. Chiefs declared certain reeftops *tabu*, or forbidden, and village elders agreed to the ban. Although it has no legal standing, villagers generally respect the decree.

The Ono Island project was established in the late '90s after a village chief attended a conservation workshop and took the lessons back to his village. He gathered agreements from villagers who fished the area and set aside two deep reeftop patches. Fishing has improved on neighboring reeftops as fish stocks have recovered. The World Wildlife Fund and the University of the South Pacific are now involved in the project.

The Taveuni project was started in the late '90s by the villagers of Waitabu (which, ironically, in Fijian means sacred or forbidden water). The effort is fund-ed by Tourism Resource Consultants, a New Zealand organization that also backs village-based tourism initiatives concerning the Bouma waterfalls and Lavena Coastal Walk on Taveuni.

Helen Sykes, a biologist involved with the project, tells the story:

"The villagers of Waitabu were interested in making a snorkeling park to attract a little tourism to their village. We set aside a 1km stretch of reeftop, and the villagers agreed on a tabu to stop all fishing, collecting and reef walking. At the start of the project, the reef had been severely damaged by traditional reef walking and overfishing. When I went back 18 months later, there were significant returns of marine life."

Villagers have since been trained as snorkel guides and now offer regular village visits and reef tours. Other villages on Taveuni have expressed interest in starting their own conservation projects, while the fight for legal protection of the reefs continues.

Responsible Diving

Dive sites are often along reefs and walls covered in beautiful corals and sponges. It only takes a moment—an inadvertently placed hand or knee, or a careless brush or kick with a fin—to destroy this fragile, living part of our delicate ecosystem. By following certain basic guidelines while diving, you can help preserve the ecology and beauty of the reefs.

1. Never drop boat anchors onto a coral reef and take care not to ground boats on coral. Encourage dive operators and regulatory bodies in their efforts to establish permanent moorings at appropriate dive sites.

2. Avoid touching living marine organisms with your body and equipment. Polyps can be damaged by even the gentlest contact. Never stand on or touch living coral. The use of gloves is no longer recommended: Gloves make it too easy to hold on to the reef. The abrasion caused by gloves may be even more damaging to the reef than your hands. If you must hold on to the reef, touch only exposed rock or dead coral.

3. Be conscious of your fins. Even without contact, the surge

Resist the temptation to buy shells.

from heavy fin strokes near the reef can do damage. Avoid full-leg kicks when diving close to the bottom and when leaving a photo scene. When you inadvertently kick something, stop kicking! It seems obvious, but some divers either panic or are totally oblivious when they bump something. When treading water in shallow reef areas, take care not to kick up clouds of sand. Settling sand can smother the delicate reef organisms.

4. Practice and maintain proper buoyancy control and avoid overweighting. Be aware that buoyancy can change over the period of an extended trip. Initially you may breathe harder and need more weighting; a few days later you may breathe more easily and need less weight. Tip: Use your weight belt and tank position to maintain a horizontal position—raise them to elevate your feet, lower them to elevate your upper body. Also be careful about buoyancy loss: As you go deeper, your wetsuit compresses, as does the air in your BC.

5. Take great care in underwater caves. Spend as little time within them as possible, as your air bubbles can damage fragile organisms. Divers should take turns inspecting the interiors of small caves or under ledges to lessen the chances of damaging contact.

6. Resist the temptation to collect or buy corals or shells. Aside from the ecological damage, collection of marine souvenirs depletes the beauty of a site and spoils others' enjoyment. The same goes for marine archaeological sites (mainly shipwrecks). Respect their integrity; some sites are even protected by law from looting.

7. Ensure that you take home all your trash and any litter you may find as well. Plastics in particular are a serious threat to marine life.

8. Resist the temptation to feed fish. You may disturb their normal eating habits, encourage aggressive behavior or feed them food that is detrimental to their health.

9. Minimize your disturbance of marine animals. Don't ride on the backs of turtles or manta rays, as this can cause them great anxiety.

Marine Conservation Organizations

Coral reefs and oceans are facing unprecedented environmental pressures. The following groups are actively involved in promoting responsible diving practices, publicizing environmental marine threats and lobbying for better policies:

CEDAM International
☎ 914-271-5365
www.cedam.org
cedamint@aol.com

CORAL: The Coral Reef Alliance
☎ 510-848-0110
www.coral.org
info@coral.org

The Cousteau Society
☎ 757-523-9335
www.cousteausociety.org
cousteau@cousteausociety.org

Greenpeace Pacific
☎ 679-312-784
www.greenpeace.org

Project AWARE Foundation
☎ 714-540-0251
www.projectaware.org
aware@padi.com

ReefKeeper International
☎ 305-358-4600
www.reefkeeper.org
reefkeeper@reefkeeper.org

Listings

Telephone Calls

To call Fiji, dial the international access code for the country you are calling from (in the U.S. it's 011) + 679 (Fiji's country code) + the 6-digit local number.

Diving Services

Some of Fiji's dive operations are owned and sometimes managed by a resort and share the same contact numbers. Others may be integrated into a resort, but are independently owned and managed. In such cases, you'll find contact information for the resort listed below under Affiliated Resort(s).

There are also a number of independent dive shops that work with hotels in their vicinity. These operators can often help you find suitable accommodations, even if they are not affiliated with a particular resort. Ask about package rates. Most operators offer pickup services to neighboring hotels and resorts.

The majority of the following dive operations offer certification and advanced or specialty diving courses. Most shops also rent or sell brand-name scuba gear and accept major credit cards. Many offer special trips, including snorkeling, surfing, fishing, shark dives, pleasure cruises and glass-bottom boat tours. Some offer E6 processing and camera and camcorder rentals, as well as underwater scooter rentals.

Viti Levu

Aqua-Trek Beqa
P.O. Box 83, Pacific Harbor, Deuba, Fiji Islands
☎ 450 324
Toll-free: ☎ 800-541-4334 (U.S.)
aquatrekbeqa@is.com.fj
www.aquatrek.com
Affiliated Resort: Centra Resort Pacific Harbor (centrapacharb@is.com.fj, www.centra.com.au)

Aqua-Trek Fiji
P.O. Box 10215, Nadi International Airport, Fiji Islands
☎ 702 413 fax: 702 412
Toll-free: ☎ 800-541-4334 (U.S.)
aquatrek@is.com.fj
www.aquatrek.com
Affiliated Resorts: Pickups available from most resorts in the area

Beqa Divers Fiji
G.P.O. Box 777, Suva, Fiji Islands
☎ 361 088 fax: 361 047
divefiji@is.com.fj
www.beqadivers.com
Affiliated Resort: Lagoon Resort (lagoon@is.com.fj)

Crystal Divers Fiji
P.O. Box 432, Rakiraki, Fiji Islands
☎ 694 747 fax: 694 877
info@crystaldivers.com
www.crystaldivers.com
Affiliated Resort: Wananavu Beach Resort (wananavuresort@is.com.fj)

Viti Levu (continued)

Dive Tropex
P.O. Box 10522, Nadi International
Airport, Fiji Islands
☎ 703 944 or 750 944 fax: 703 955
divetropex@is.com.fj
www.divetropex.com
Affiliated Resorts: Sheraton Fiji Resort
(☎ 750 777), Sheraton Royal Denarau
(☎ 750 000), Treasure Island Resort
(treasureisland@is.com.fj, www.treasure
.com.fj), Tokoriki Island Resort (tokoriki
@is.com.fj, www.tokoriki.com)

Marlin Bay Resort
Box 112, Deuba, Fiji Islands
☎ 304 042 fax: 304 028
Toll-free: ☎ 800-542-3454 (U.S.)
marlinbay-reservation@worldnet
.att.net
www.marlinbay.com

Pro Dive Fiji
P.O. Box 123, Korolevu, Fiji Islands
☎ 530 199 fax: 530 300
prodivefiji@is.com.fj
www.prodivefiji.com
Affiliated Resort: The Warwick Fiji
(warwickres@is.com.fj, www.warwick
fiji.com); pickups available from The
Naviti Resort, Hideaway Resort,
Tambua Sands Beach Resort and
Crusoe's Retreat

Ra Divers
P.O. Box 417, Rakiraki, Fiji Islands
☎ 694 511 fax: 694 611
radivers@is.com.fj

www.radivers.com
Affiliated Resort: Wananavu Beach
Resort (wananavuresort@is.com.fj);
pickups available from various backpacker resorts on Nananu-i-ra

Scuba Bula
P.O. Box 9530, Nadi International
Airport, Fiji Islands
☎ 706 100 fax: 706 094
seashell@is.com.fj
www.scubabula.com
Affiliated Resort: Seashell Cove Resort
(seashell@is.com.fj, www.seashell
resort.com)

Sonaisali Island Resort Fiji
P.O. Box 2544, Nadi, Fiji Islands
☎ 706 011 fax: 706 092
info@sonaisali.com
www.sonaisali.com

Toberua Island Resort
P.O. Box 567, Suva, Fiji Islands
☎ 302 356 fax: 302 215
Toll-free: ☎ 800-441-6880 (U.S.)
toberua@is.com.fj
www.toberua.com

Vatulele Island Resort
P.O. Box 9936, Nadi International
Airport, Fiji Islands
☎ 720 300 fax: 720 062
☎ +61 02-9665 8700 (international)
Toll-free: ☎ 800-828-9146 (U.S.)
vatulele@is.com.fj
www.vatulele.com

Mamanuca & Yasawa Groups

Aqua-Trek Mana
P.O. Box 10215, Nadi International
Airport, Fiji Islands
☎ 669 309
Toll-free: ☎ 800-541-4334 (U.S.)
aquatrek@is.com.fj
www.aquatrek.com
Affiliated Resort: Mana Island Resort
(mana@is.com.fj,
www.bulafiji.com/web/mana)

Aqua-Trek Matamanoa
P.O. Box 10215, Nadi International
Airport, Fiji Islands
☎ 669 309
Toll-free: ☎ 800-541-4334 (U.S.)
aquatrek@is.com.fj
www.aquatrek.com
Affiliated Resort: Matamanoa Island
Resort (matamanoa@is.com.fj,
www.bulafiji.com/web/matamanoa)

Mamanuca & Yasawa Groups (continued)

Castaway Diving
Private Mailbag, Nadi International
Airport, Fiji Islands
☎ 661 233 fax: 665 753
dive@castawayfiji.com.fj
www.castawayfiji.com
Affiliated Resort: Castaway Island
Resort (castawayfiji@is.com.fj)

Subsurface Fiji
P.O. Box 1626, Lautoka, Fiji Islands
☎ 666 738 fax: 669 955
subsurface@fijidiving.com
www.fijidiving.com
Affiliated Resorts: Beachcomber Island
Resort (beachcomber@is.com.fj,
www.beachcomber.com), Musket
Cove Resort (musketcovefiji@is.com.fj,
www.musketcovefiji.com); pickups
available from Lako Mai, Malolo
Island, Namotu Island, Navini Island,
Tavarua Island and Wadigi Island
resorts

West Side Water Sports
P.O. Box 7136, Lautoka, Fiji Islands
☎ 661 462
westside@is.com.fj
www.fiji-dive.com
Affiliated Resorts: Most resorts in the
nearby Yasawas, including Otto &
Fanny Doughty's, Turtle Island and
Blue Lagoon Cruises

Yasawa Island Resort
P.O. Box 10128, Nadi International
Airport, Fiji Islands
☎ 663 364 or 722 266 fax: 665 044 or
724 456
yasawa@is.com.fj
yasawaisland@is.com.fj
www.yasawa.com

Vanua Levu & Namena

Eco Divers-Tours
P.O. Box 264, Savusavu, Fiji Islands
☎ 850 122 fax: 850 344
ecodivers@is.com.fj
www.bulafiji.com/web/ecodiver
Affiliated Resort: Koro Sun Resort
(info@korosunresort.com, www.koro
sunresort.com)

L'Aventure Jean-Michel Cousteau Fiji
c/o Jean-Michel Cousteau Fiji Islands
Resort
Post Office, Savusavu, Fiji Islands
☎ 850 188 fax: 850 340

laventurefiji@is.com.fj
www.jmcfir.com
Affiliated Resort: Jean-Michel
Cousteau Fiji Islands Resort
(info@fijiresort.com,
www.fijiresort.com)

Moody's Namena
Private Mailbag, Savusavu, Fiji Islands
☎ 813 764 fax: 812 366
moodysnamena@is.com.fj
www.bulafiji.com/web/moodys

Taveuni

Aqua-Trek Taveuni
P.O. Box 1, Waiyevo, Taveuni,
Fiji Islands
☎ 880 286 fax: 880 288
Toll-free: ☎ 800-541-4334 (U.S.)
garden@is.com.fj
www.aquatrek.com
Affiliated Resort: Garden Island Resort
(garden@is.com.fj)

Aquaventure
P.A. Matei, Taveuni, Fiji Islands
☎ 880 381
aquaventure@is.com.fj
www.aquaventure.org
Affiliated Resorts: Pickups available
from most nearby resorts

Taveuni (continued)

Dive Taveuni
P.A. Matei, Taveuni, Fiji Islands
☎ 880 441 fax: 880 466
divetaveuni@divetaveuni.com
www.divetaveuni.com
Affiliated Resort: Taveuni Island Resort
(www.taveuniislandresort.com)

Swiss Fiji Divers
P.A. Matei, Taveuni, Fiji Islands
☎ 880 586
sfd@is.com.fj
www.swissfijidivers.com
Affiliated Resort: Maravu Plantation
Resort (maravu@is.com.fj,
www.maravu.com)

Tropical Dive
P.O. Box 83, Waiyevo, Taveuni,
Fiji Islands
☎ 880 260/776 fax: 880 274
tropicaldive@divefiji.com
www.divefiji.com
Affiliated Resort: Matangi Island
Resort (matangiisland@is.com.fj,
www.matangiisland.com)

Vuna Reef Divers
P.O. Box 69, Waiyevo, Taveuni,
Fiji Islands
☎ 880 531/125
Affiliated Resort: Susie's Plantation
Resort (susies@is.com.fj)

Kadavu Group

Dive Kadavu
P.O. Box 8, Vunisea, Kadavu,
Fiji Islands
☎ 311 780 fax: 303 860

divekadavu@is.com.fj
www.divekadavu.com
Affiliated Resort: Matana Beach Resort
(divekadavu@is.com.fj)

Lomaiviti Group

Ovalau Watersports Fiji
P.O. Box 149, Levuka, Ovalau,
Fiji Islands
☎ 440 611 fax: 440 405
dive@owlfiji.com
www.owlfiji.com
Affiliated Resort: Ovalau Holiday
Resort (info@ohrfiji.com,
www.ohrfiji.com)

Tropical Dive
P.A. Matei, Taveuni, Fiji Islands
☎ 880 776
tropicaldive@divefiji.com
www.divefiji.com
Affiliated Resort: Naigani Island Resort
naigani@is.com.fj,
www.bulafiji.com/web/naigani)

Lau Group

Lomaloma Resort
P.O. Box 55, Lomaloma, Vanua Balavu,
Fiji Islands

☎ 880 446 fax: 880 303
lomaloma@is.com.fj
www.lomalomaresort.com

Live-Aboards

Fiji Aggressor

Fiji Aggressor Ltd., P.O. Box 3174, Lami, Suva, Fiji Islands
☎ 361 382 or 998 821 fax: 362 930
Toll-free: ☎ 800-344-5662 or 800-348-2628 (U.S.)
fijiaggressor@is.com.fj
www.aggressor.com
Home Port: Denarau
Description: 32m (105ft) aluminum catamaran
Destinations: E6, Mount Mutiny (Hi8), Namena, Wakaya
Duration: 7 days (diving and shore excursions)
Passengers: 16
Other: E6 processing available, nitrox

MV *Princess II*

☎ 725 116 fax: 725 220
Toll-free: ☎ 800-576-7327 (U.S.)
info@princessii.com
www.princessii.com
Home Port: Denarau
Description: 26m (85ft) steel monohull
Destinations: E6, Namena, Somo-somo, Matagi, northern Lau Group
Duration: 7 days; other itineraries upon request
Passengers: 12

Nai'a

Nai'a Cruises Fiji, P.O. Box 332, Pacific Harbour, Fiji Islands
☎ 450 382 fax: 450 566
Toll-free: ☎ 800-903-0272 (U.S.)
naia@is.com.fj
www.naia.com.fj
Home Port: Lautoka
Description: 37m (120ft) steel monohull
Destinations: Bligh Water, Namena, Wakaya, Gau; special trips to Tonga and Vanuatu
Duration: 7 or 10 days
Passengers: 18
Other: E6 processing available, nitrox

Sere-ni-Wai

Mollie Dean Cruises, P.O. Box 3256, Lami, Suva, Fiji Islands
☎ 361 171 fax: 361 137
sere@is.com.fj
www.sere.com.fj
Home Port: Suva
Description: 31m (101ft) steel/aluminum monohull
Destinations: Namena, E6, Wakaya
Duration: 7 or 10 nights
Passengers: 10

Visitors Bureaus

Contact the following agencies for more information on Fiji, or visit the Fiji Visitors Bureau online at www.bulafiji.com:

Fiji

Nadi
Fiji Visitors Bureau
Nadi International Airport concourse
Box 9217, Nadi International Airport,
Fiji Islands
☎ 722 433 fax: 720 141
fvbnadi@is.com.fj
Note: This office is open extended
hours and meets all international flights

Suva
Fiji Visitors Bureau
Thomson Street
G.P.O. Box 92, Suva, Fiji Islands
☎ 302 433 fax: 300 970 or 302 751
infodesk@fijifvb.gov.fj

Index

dive sites covered in this book appear in **bold** type

Lonely Planet Pisces Books

The **Diving & Snorkeling** guides cover top destinations worldwide. Beautifully illustrated with full-color photos throughout, the series explores the best diving and snorkeling areas and prepares divers for what to expect when they get there. Each site is described in detail, with information on suggested ability levels, depth, visibility and, of course, marine life. There's basic topside information as well for each destination.

Also check out dive guides to:

Lonely Planet

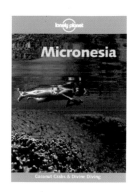

travel guidebooks	in-depth coverage with background and recommendations
shoestring guides	for those with plenty of time and limited money
condensed guides	highlight the best a destination has to offer
citySync	digital city guides for Palm™ OS
outdoor guides	walking, cycling, diving and watching wildlife series
phrasebooks	including unusual languages and two-way dictionaries
city maps and road atlases	essential navigation tools
world food	explores local cuisine and produce
out to eat	a city's best places to eat and drink
read this first	invaluable pre-departure guides
healthy travel	practical advice for staying well on the road
journeys	great reading for armchair explorers
pictorial	lavishly illustrated coffee table books
ekno	low-cost phonecard with e-services
TV series and videos	stories from on the road
website	for chat, upgrades, and up-to-date destination facts
lonely planet images	online photo library

Download free guidebook upgrades at:
www.lonelyplanet.com

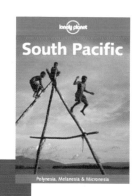

Lonely Planet Publications

Australia
Locked Bag 1, Footscray, Victoria, 3011
☎ (03) 9689 4666 fax: (03) 9689 6833
email: talk2us@lonelyplanet.com.au

USA
150 Linden Street
Oakland, California 94607
☎ (510) 893 8555, (800) 275 8555
fax: (510) 893 8563
email: info@lonelyplanet.com

UK
10a Spring Place,
London NW5 3BH
☎ (0171) 428 4800 fax: (0171) 428 4828
email: go@lonelyplanet.co.uk

France
1 rue du Dahomey
75011 Paris
☎ 01 55 25 33 00 fax: 01 55 25 33 01
email: bip@lonelyplanet.fr

www.lonelyplanet.com